Transformation: From the Inside Out

Sister2Sistah

A Collection of Stories Women Have Faced & Conquered

Transformation: From the Inside Out

Managing Editor
Notoshia D. Howard

Transformation: From the Inside Out

© 2016 Howard Publishing Press LLC

All rights reserved. This book is protected by the copyright laws of the United States of America. This book may not be copied or reprinted for commercial gain or profit. Content and/or cover may not be reproduced in whole or in part in any form without the written consent of the authors or publisher.

Scripture quotations taken from the Comparative Study Bible NIV, Amplified, KJV and Updated NASB. Copyright © 1999 by Zondervan.

Scripture quotations taken from (NLT) are taken from the Holy Bible, New Living Translation, copyright © 1996. Used by permission of Tyndale House Publishers, Inc., Wheaton, Illinois 60189. All rights reserved.

Howard Publishing Press LLC
"We Publish the Gift that God Has Given You."
Phone: 317-529-9562
Email: howardpublishing@sbcglobal.net
Website: www.howardpublishingpress.com

Book cover design by: Kevin Essett
Editor: Danielle Love
Sister2Sistah: Transformation From the Inside Out.

ISBN: 978-0-9909972-7-6

Printed in the United States of America

Dedication

This book is dedicated to all the women who have been hurt, abused, sick, or have felt neglected, or as if there is no help or nobody cares. This book is dedicated to our African-American sisters, European sisters, Asian sisters, Hispanic sisters, our rich sisters, poor sisters, middle-class sisters, stepsisters, sisters-in-law, half-sisters, play sisters, our quiet sisters and our loud sisters.

This book is devoted to letting our sistahs know that we got their back. We are praying for you, encouraging you, supporting you, and we love you. Even though we are not born by the same mother and father we are connected through love. It's love that gives us the strength and the courage to support and praise you to your destiny. We as women have enough enemies, and so it is time to bond together.

Just as cancer has no racial barriers, death has no racial barriers, rejection and abuse have no racial barriers or economic limits. No one is exempt from death, hurt, pain, denial, depression, anxiety, cancer, abuse or drugs.

We women all have a story. Sometimes our ending is good and sometimes our ending is not so good. Yet it is not what you're going through that counts, but instead it is how you handle what you are going through and who you have become at the end of the day. Are you the woman that cries wolf or the woman that gives up? Or are you the woman that has taken all of her hurts, pain and experiences and given them into the hands of the one that can do something about it?

Sister, we want you to know that you are a beautiful queen. We love you and you are the apple of our Father's eye; He loves you and will never give up on you.

Transformation: From the Inside Out

Transformation: From the Inside Out

Table of Contents

INTRODUCTION - Prophetess Rachel Sanders	11
Kizzy Hayes Broken to be Blessed	13
Marian Steele If He Did it Before, He Can Do it Again	27
Trease Sears The Independent Married Woman	41
Schurronda White Stepping Out	57
Roberta Bell A Love Story	71
Brittany Sullivan Stuck: Inside of Who She is, Who She Was, and Who She is Becoming	89
Peggy Finkton The Journey	119
Michele Miller A Look Back to Move Forward	129
Notoshia D. Howard Rejected but Anointed	143

Transformation: From the Inside Out

Endorsement

If there was one word that I would use regarding the few stories that I read within *Sister2Sistah*, it would be WOW! Wow is a way of saying "way over wonderful". It is an exclamation of delight, surprise and amazement. These powerful women ought to be commended for opening up their lives to complete strangers. These stories will help many people that the authors will never meet. It feels good to know that there are women still willing to help another sistah out.

While reading these very personal stories, I felt a sense of relief. To know that I am not the only one who has personal struggles. It was confirmed that I am not an outcast, abnormal, or alone. These stories prove that there are mothers, wives, and daughters that have experienced very similar moments that I have.

I read "If He Did It Before, He Can Do It Again", "The Independent Married Woman", "Broken to be Blessed" and "Stepping Out". These stories prove that God is truly amazing. The healing and deliverance that has taken place in the lives of these women are true and living testimonies. Every woman, regardless of what stage of life they are in, need to get this book. These stories will assure you that you can overcome any and every situation.

Lady Selena C. Woods
Rhema Life Church

Endorsement

    Sister2Sistah is a must read for every woman! These women walked down different paths but all ended up giving their situations to God! By doing so God healed them spiritually, physically and mentally. This book is about real women with real issues. As I was reading each one of their stories, I felt encouraged. I saw how God was working in their lives from the very beginning of each trial that they went through. I loved the honesty of each one on how they felt as they were dealing with each of their situations. It was real raw emotions, which a lot of us have felt or may be feeling right now. I am so thankful for their honesty to share their story and I know many lives will be touched and changed because of their courage to share this awesome book with us. I know that mine has...

Evangelist Julie LaPorta

Endorsement

This book is filled to the point of overflow with one thing....TRANSPARENCY.

Each story makes you feel as if you are a part of the cast of characters while causing you to think of your own personal similarities and parallels.

I found myself cheering for each writer and looking forward to reading the conclusion of her experience, knowing that it would leave me filled with hope, inspiration, faith and tenacity. The stories aren't written in some sort of theological or literary "code" that will take you weeks to interpret, but in everyday language that draws you in and touches your soul...even after you've finished reading them.

What an empowering and liberating reading experience I believe this book will be to its many readers...I know it was for me.

Tara Thompson
Global Harvest Christian Center, Pastor

Endorsement

    Sister2Sistah is a book that is a true God sent! Are you in need of a reminder of the power of God and that His Grace is sufficient? Then, these glorious testimonies of these strong women will have you wanting to tell others about the wondrous works of God.

Venessa Sallie
 The Author of: *Trapped*

INTRODUCTION

As we all look around in today's society, we notice a paradigm shift that's taking place all across the land. Where there used to be unity, love and concern for one another, now we look around and we will notice that we are all doing our own thing; we all are holding in what God is or has done in our lives. We don't share what God is or has been doing with us. However, I thank God for the writers of *Sister2Sistah*. I thank God for these women defying the odds, coming on one accord, listening to the voice of God and making the step to share with us publicly what God has done for them privately.

Throughout this reading, you will find a compilation of stories of how one sister went from being broken to being blessed, you will read testimonies of how God took someone from the world's standards of nothing and showed her that she's *worth* something. You will read how these women decide to step out on faith and trust God in all that they do. You will see that they all serve the same God and that this God is the same yesterday, today and forevermore. Despite what they are going through, despite what they have been through—that if He's done it before He can do it again. This reading will make you laugh and it will make you cry, but most of all it will show you the hand of God moving in the lives of these women.

This reading will not only enlighten you, but it will bless you. It will open doors for some and shut doors for others. Scripture says that we are overcome by the word of our testimony and it's through the testimony of these ladies that you will see that God is still a miracle worker.

Transformation: From the Inside Out

    I pray that you will be blessed, and I pray that you will also understand that as we grow in grace, whatever it is God has or is doing for you, share your story. Share your testimony, because you never know how your story or your testimony may be the catalyst to push someone closer to Christ.

    May God bless you for your support and may you find favor from this day forth.

Prophetess Rachel L. Sanders
WOMAN2WOMAN Women's Ministry
Author of: *And HE is my Source*

About the Author

Ms. Kizzy Hayes

Kizzy Hayes is the baby of thirteen children. She was born and raised in Gulfport, Mississippi. Kizzy moved to Indianapolis, Indiana in September of 2008. She is currently employed with the State of Indiana and was previously employed with the State of Mississippi for ten years. She is the mother of three wonderful children whose names are Destiny, Cardale and Barrington. Kizzy loves to shop and travel and has been blessed to visit the Bahamas, Cozumel, Belize and Cancún. She plans to take a vacation to Paris very soon. She has a Bachelor's degree in Business Administration, specializing in Human Resources. Kizzy is currently attending school to pursue a degree in Business Law and become an attorney. Her passion is helping women and children who are in need; whether it is physically, mentally or financially. She is a very spiritual person because she knows God is real. She would not be the woman she is today if it were not for God's grace and mercy.

Transformation: From the Inside Out

Transformation: From the Inside Out

Acknowledgements

I would like to thank my family, friends, Apostle Jacquelyn Powell and church family for always being there to support me.

I would like to thank my mother, Iola McGowan, for always being a great mother, friend and role model. She has always been the rock of our family. Thank you, mother, for being the great woman God has designed you to be. I am very grateful to have a mother like you. Love you.

I would like to thank my children Destiny McInnis, Cardale Hayes, and Barrington Hayes for always giving me a reason to be a better person each day. I thank God for blessing me with three beautiful children like you all.

I would like to thank my best friend, Nikki Gurley, for being such a wonderful friend. You have always been there for me. I have never had to question your loyalty. We have laughed together, cried together, vacationed together and shopped together and I could not have asked for better person to share this friendship with. I can honestly say I am grateful for a friend like you. Thank you for always being that friend I can depend on.

I would like to thank my sister, Rotunda (Puney) Montgomery, for always being that rock in my life. Anyone that knows us knows that she and I cannot stand to be together, but we cannot stand to be apart. She is the ying to my yang. Most people cannot say Kizzy without saying Puney. She has always been that shoulder I could cry on, even if she was the one who caused me to cry. My sister has always been my biggest supporter. She is a true definition of being her sister's keeper.

I would like to thank my friend, Aunt Cathy Morgan, for being such a great friend and role model in my life. I can remember when you and I first met working at South Mississippi Regional Center. I was this twenty-year-old who was pregnant with my second child, and you said to me, "Baby, do not keep having all them babies at a young age. Your vagina is made to pee out of, not to keep having babies out of." Although I was married, I was scared to get pregnant

Transformation: From the Inside Out

again after you said that to me. I thank you for being that role model I could look up to and try to model. It's great women like yourself that I look up to and admire.

Transformation: From the Inside Out

Broken to be Blessed

Who Am I?

I know who the world says I am, but God, who am I?

According to the world, I am a divorced, single mother of three children who is over the age of thirty, still trying to figure out what I want out of life. Some see me as this strong black woman who has it all together. Well let me tell you right now, I am so far from having it all together. Let me share with you a little about who I was, and who God has designed me to become.

Growing up as a child and young adult, I did things that I look back on now and say, "But God!" Many who see my walk do not see what I have gone through. On the outside looking in, yes, it may have seemed like I had it all together. For instance, I lived in the big houses, drove the nice cars, and wore the nice clothes and shoes. But many people do not realize what I did to get those things. I think back to when I was out there in the crack houses, hanging out with drug dealers, or when I had a gambling addiction. I also think about when my lights were being cut off, not having money to feed my children, and being too ashamed to ask my family for help. I also think about when I was out there writing bad checks or going into stores changing price tags on clothes so my kids could have the things I thought they deserved.

I often asked myself, *who am I?* Then, one day, I began to pray on my way to work. My prayer to God was no longer "who am I", but "God, make me into the woman you have designed me to become." I trusted God enough to know that if I became the woman he designed me to become, I would be nothing but greatness. My walk with God has not been easy, but it has been worth it. God delivered me from gambling, he removed those people I surrounded myself with people who did not mean me any good. When I left Mississippi in September of 2008, I came to Indiana with my truck, some clothes, and my three kids. I had no job, no money and no place to live. But I trusted God enough to know he would supply all me and my kids' needs. My three kids and I moved in with my sister and her daughter in a two-bedroom apartment. There I was, this divorced mother of three kids, no job, no money and no place to call my own. I found myself crying many days, asking myself what I have gotten myself into. Nevertheless, I kept praying and trusting in God that me and my kids' needs would be supplied.

I remember going in the Welfare office to apply for Cash Assistance, Food Stamps, and Medicaid. The caseworker sent me to an impact class for job assessment training. I remember sitting in class thinking, *I do not need this class I know how to fill out an application and how to dress for an interview*. I wanted to quit, but this was nothing but a set-up from God. After I completed the job assessment training, I was hired as a caseworker with the Welfare office and then later became a manager over the Welfare office. All I can say is, "but God!"

God has taken a nobody and has gradually designed me into somebody. When I moved to Indiana, I only had a high school diploma, no money, three kids all under the age of ten, no place to live, and no job! Well, I am here to tell you God has supplied all me and my kids' needs. I am currently an owner of a four-bedroom home that is fully furnished. I have not just a job, but a career. I graduated from college with my second degree in May of 2016. My daughter is a high school graduate who is attending college. God has made me the lender and not the borrower. I am grateful for the woman that God is designing me to become. I no longer ask who I am because I know I am, a woman who is being designed by God!

Transformation: From the Inside Out

"Being Redeemed from Soul Ties"

People who have many past relationships find it very difficult to 'bond' or join to anybody, because their souls are fragmented. I did not realize this until I became single and started dating. I remember dating a man who was good to me but was not good for me. Let me explain, this man was married, but I did not care. I felt like my marriage did not work, so I did not care about anyone else's marriage. I know this may sound crazy, but at that point in my life, I had begun to accept craziness. The devil had me out there so bad, not caring about who I hurt. When you are in a place of hurt and disappointment, the devil will use what he can to distract you from God's purpose for your life. When a person has ungodly sexual relations with another person, an ungodly soul tie is then formed, "What? Know ye not that he which is joined to a harlot is one body? For two, saith he, shall be one flesh." (1 Corinthians 6:16, KJV).

I was this twenty-seven-year old, divorced mother who felt like my world that I once knew no longer existed. You see, I dated only one guy from the age of thirteen up until we got married right out of high school. I did not have very much experience with dating, and all I wanted was for someone to love me. No matter the cost or who it might hurt.

This man and I dated for a couple of years, and I felt like it was perfect because I saw him when it was convenient for the both of us. He took me on vacations and bought me nice things, but I did not realize those things came with a cost. I was selling my soul to the devil without even realizing it.

This man gave me what I thought I needed in a relationship despite the fact he was there part-time. I was in a place in my life where there was emptiness, and I wanted it filled. I felt like this man was all I needed in a relationship. I was so content with being the other woman. My favorite saying was, "I don't want anyone unless they have someone." I was lost out there in this world. Although I knew better, I was in a place of hurt and bitterness.

Transformation: From the Inside Out

Hurt and bitterness is the worst place to be in life. I remember praying and asking God for this man to leave his wife to be with me. Yes, I said it, I wanted God to break up a marriage for my selfish ways. I allowed this man to impregnate my mind with the lies and deceptions. I went into this relationship being content with being the other woman by being deceived by what I thought was a perfect relationship. I never considered the fact that this man had a wife and family. All I cared about was how he made me feel as a woman, and that was good enough for me. I remember him promising me he was going to leave his wife to be with me.

He eventually left his wife to be with me and other women too! I guess like that old saying goes: "if he cheats on her to be with you, he will cheat on you to be with someone else." My life was once again a living hell! This married man was still sleeping with his wife, me and other women too! I remember asking him why he was sleeping with other women, and he told me, "When I am with you, I am with you. Do not question me about who I am with when I am not with you." I left one bad relationship to be in another relationship with someone who really was not mine to begin with.

I remember going to church, and it was like God was using the preacher to speak directly to me. The preacher said, "Many of you are here praying and asking God for someone else's husband or wife, but how many of you know that what God joined together no man can separate?" Many of you are in relationships that are unequally yoked, and you wonder why you are going through hell with that person. Ungodly soul ties fragments the soul and is destructive. I began to cry, because I knew God had greater for me. This relationship was not what God had joined together, how could I expect for it to be blessed?

I began to pray and ask God to remove this man from me. Yes, the same man whose marriage I wanted God to break up for me is the same man I was asking God to remove out of my life. A lot of times we pray and ask God for people and things that do not mean us any good. It took me five years to get this man out of my system. Although I knew he did not mean me any good, I was still unable to end this relationship. Not realizing we had soul ties, I did not understand why my mind craved for this man. Sleeping with this man, I allowed a part of his soul to enter in my body. I began to take on his ways of lying, cheating, and being deceitful.

I began to jump from one relationship to another. This was my second time being hurt, and I refused to allow myself to be hurt again. I guess I was what they call a "woman scorned". I was headed for destruction. After finally leaving this toxic relationship, I prayed and asked God to allow me to be happy with being by myself. I felt that in order for me to get what God has for me, I needed to repent for committing adultery and having sex before marriage. I spoke this verbally "I now rebuke and bind any ungodly soul ties formed between myself and _____ as a result of _____ (fornication, adultery, etc.) in Jesus' name, Amen!" Then, I got rid of gifts that were given to me in connection with sin or unholy relationships. I felt holding on to those things symbolized an ungodly relationship, and would hold a soul tie in place. While I do not think it is always necessary to destroy all the gifts and things that you have been given during a relationship, I would not encourage you to hang on to such things that symbolize sin.

The devil thought he had me, but God kept me in spite of my foolish ways. I no longer count on someone else to make me happy, because I know with God's love and guidance the right man will come into my life!

We as women have to realize our worth and not jump into bed or a relationship with every man that has "breath and britches" as my grandmother used to say. Ladies, we have to realize God created us to be a good thing to man and to obtain favor from the Lord. The Lord did not create a woman to be a baby mama, side chick, mistress, or anything other than being a good thing to her husband. Once we realize our worth and seek God, your husband will find you, not you find him. I love the story of Ruth and Boaz in the Bible. Many of us often say, "Lord, send me my Boaz", but often times we do not want to have the faith and discipline that Ruth had.

Transformation: From the Inside Out

I am learning how to be the woman God has called me to be. Because the Bible says in Proverbs 18:22 *"A man who finds a wife finds a good thing and obtains favor from the Lord."* I want to be my husband's good thing, which causes him to obtain favor from the Lord. During this process of being single, instead of trying to be every man's good thing, I choose to wait on the Lord to send me my husband, so I can be his good thing.

"Don't Confuse the Process with the Purpose God Has for Your Life"

Have you ever just wondered what your purpose is here on Earth? This is something I struggled with for a long time. I did not know what my purpose was in life. I went to work, church, school, and home. On the weekends, I may hang out with friends sometimes, I never really felt like I had a purpose here on Earth. You see, when people see me, they assume I am this outgoing person. In reality, I was a mess on the inside. I felt lost in this world. Many times, I thought about just ending my life. I did not realize I was only going through the process that God had ordained over my life.

Let me explain, when I was a year old I had to have open-heart surgery. The doctors told my mother to call the family in, because I was not going to make it through the night. Mother said she went to the chapel and fell on her knees and prayed. She told God, "This is your child and I give her back to you." After leaving the chapel, my mother went back up to my room. The doctors said to my mother, "I do not know what is going on, but your child is breathing on her own. If she makes it through the night, we will take her off the ventilator." Lying in that hospital bed at a young age, the Lord healed my body. The doctors did not understand how I went from not breathing on my own to breathing without a ventilator. This was only the process God had ordained over my life. My mother knew I would be healed, because she understood the purpose God had for my life.

Transformation: From the Inside Out

The doctors told my mother I would have to come back for surgery at the age of thirteen because the artificial valves they put in my heart would have to be replaced. They also told my mother I would have seizures and take medication for the rest of my life.

Well, I am here to tell you I am thirty-seven years old and I have never had to have surgery again. When I went for my check up at the age of thirteen, the doctors said it was a miracle because my valves had grown over the artificial valves they put in me when I was a year old. I have never had to take any medication, nor have I had any seizures since I left the hospital as a child. The devil thought he was going to take me out at a young age. I did not know my purpose here on Earth, but the Lord knew what my purpose was. He saved me so I could be a testimony of His healing power.

Then as an adult the devil has tried everything he knew to destroy me. I have been lied on, talked about and used by people I thought had my best interest at heart. I remember crying many days, wondering why people would lie on me or talk about me without knowing me. I did not understand this was only a process I was going through because God had a purpose for my life. Everyone has their own walk in life. My walk has not always been easy, but God has allowed me to continue to walk this path in life. I know how it feels to have your lights cut off or be evicted from your home. Going through that process in my life developed me into the woman I am today. I know to pay my bills before I go spend money on foolish things. I think about when I used to hide my car from the repo man or dodge the property owner because I spent my money on foolish things. I thank God for that process I went through in my life because without going through that process, I would not be grateful for what God has blessed me with. When you go without, you learn how to appreciate when you get it again.

I learned that you cannot be who God called you to be and still keep all the same friends and habits; elevation requires separation of people and things that do not mean you any good. Often times, our purpose in life can be sidetracked by the things and people we have around us. Everyone who calls you their friend does not always have your best interest at heart. Be careful who you confide in. In the Bible, it spoke about Jesus being betrayed by Judas. My prayer to God is. "God, please remove anything or anyone away from me that does not mean me any good."

I remember when I first prayed that prayer, and God started revealing things and people who did not mean me any good. People I had known for a very long time, God began to reveal to me their true intentions. All my life, I was taught to be a giver and when I no longer had anything to offer, those people began to flee. At first, it was hard for me to let those people and things go, because I was afraid of being alone. I have learned to trust God with His purpose He has over my life.

Since then, my life has been so much happier. I now go to bed in peace and wake up in peace. I am not saying my life is perfect, I am just saying I have learned how to fight my battles. Life is just like preparing for a test in school. Before you take the test, you must go over the material and resources. I have learned to listen to the instructions and use the resources that God has given me to go through the process so I can redeem the purpose He has for my life!

Autograph Page

Ms. Kizzy Hayes

Transformation: From the Inside Out

About the Author
Mrs. Marian V. Steele

Sis. Marian V. Steele is a member of Calvary Baptist Church of Chicago, where the Rev. Dr. James R. Flint, Jr. is the Pastor. She is the wife of Rev. Robert Steele, who she has been married to for twenty-five years. They are both Co-Directors for the Calvary's Children Church. Sis. Steele is also a Sunday School Teen teacher and works with the church's women's ministry. Sis. Steele has been employed with the State of Illinois' Child Support Division for forty years, where she has served in several different capacities. Currently, she is an Outreach Specialist, where she often speaks to teen parents, women's shelters, men's groups, homeless veterans and others about the services the agency offers. Sis. Steele believes that serving God's people in your secular position is just as important as in your Christian position.

Her true love is working for and nurturing God's people. She loves working with children and youth, but her true desire is to minister to women in need. She and her husband are the founders of their new ministry *"Steele on the Move for Christ Ministry"*. Their motto is: *"Serving God's People as He Would have Them Served"*. She feels that our true purpose in life is to teach God's Word to the lost and to those in need, helping them to know of God's great sacrifice for mankind.

Transformation: From the Inside Out

Sis. Steele stated that if she had to share one scripture with someone it would be: Matthew 6:33—"But Seek ye first, the kingdom of God, and his righteousness and all these things shall be added unto you."

Acknowledgements

I am so grateful for this opportunity to share with others how God has blessed me through my journey.

I would especially like to thank my BEST friend, my husband, Rev. Robert Steele. He has been so kind and understanding as I worked on my manuscript through some late nights, giving up his dinner and honey time with me.

I would like to thank Prophetess Rachel Sanders for introducing me to Pastor Notoshia Howard. This is the beginning of a loving sistership.

Thank you Pastor Notoshia Howard for this great opportunity allowing me to share with someone that just might not know, that if He did it before, He can do it again.

And last but not least, I would like to say thank you to my Pastor, Rev. Dr. James R. Flint, Jr., for his spiritual words of direction through his preaching and teaching from the pulpit.

Transformation: From the Inside Out

Transformation: From the Inside Out

If He did it before, He can do it again

"But seek ye first the kingdom of God, and his righteousness; and all these things shall be added unto you." (Matthew 6:33, KJV).

When I look at Matthew 6:33 and think of the meaning, I say to myself that God is telling me to seek Him for a carefree life. I can even go as far as to say, He promised to never leave me alone. Well, I asked myself, *does this mean I will never see storms in my life?* Absolutely not! My pastor once said in his sermon that, "God's peace doesn't mean the absence of trouble, but the presence of God's grace." I am so grateful for His grace and peace.

Even during His grace and peace, sometimes the enemy will try to distract you when you are working for the Lord. My husband and I had become Sunday school teachers at our church and were working with a few of the church ministries. On June 28, 1998, my husband accepted his calling as a Minister for God. I remember the comment said to me by a friend, to be watchful because the enemy was upset with us and might turn up the heat. Not knowing what she meant at the time, but I soon found out. Two months later, I experienced one of the greatest tests of times that I thought I would experience.

In August of 1998, my life seemed to change one day right before my eyes. After a series of medical tests I had taken, I went to my doctor's office for the results. He informed me my results showed I had breast cancer. I remember having a small piece of string in my hand at that time, folding it back and forward around my finger. It appeared to get tighter as I listened to the doctor. My husband was unable to attend my appointment with me, so I was alone at the time. I really didn't know how to respond. I didn't know how to react. Do I cry? Do I call my husband? What questions should I ask next? Should I get a second opinion from another medical facility? Was this a dream? NO, THIS WAS A NIGHTMARE! I became frightened and thought to myself, *I'll just go home and prepare for the worst.* All kinds of thoughts began to run through my mind. Even though I had faith in God, for that moment, I was losing it. I was quickly becoming unraveled and for what? Had I forgotten who I was and who my Father was? Yes, for a brief moment I had.

So I went home and got on my knees beside my bed and I cried. I was truly frightened and I wasn't sure what to do next. I remember crying and telling God I was afraid and I didn't want to die. Pleading for Him to spare my life, wanting a chance to be a better person. I was wondering if I was being punished for something I had done. At this time of my life, I was truly without words. I became upset, sad and angry. If I was being punished, what about all those people that have done things worse than me? I was not a murderer, thief or a bank robber. My mind had lost it. I had forgotten where my true peace lied. Nevertheless, I was going to soon find out. I remember telling my husband when he came home. He didn't let it bother him that much. He just wanted to know what the next step was, where do we go from here. He kept a peaceful demeanor and mind. That was probably the best thing for me at that time.

    I decided to seek a second opinion from another medical source to see if they agreed with my doctor. I contacted a nearby medical university and was given an appointment to see an Oncologist. After having a series of tests with them and consultation, they agreed that it was breast cancer and I needed surgery soon. During my appointment at the University, I found out that not only was the doctor a top Oncologist, but she was the Chief of Oncology, the head person. I remember being asked how I got an appointment with her. God had blessed me to receive my second opinion from the best in the field. I felt God knew this would give me some peace and reassurance of His presence in my life. After this, I could later see God's work unfolding in my life. But my mind was still somewhat unsettled. I began to hate the word cancer. I knew what it could do and what it had done to loved ones. I didn't like to use the word in my vocabulary. In addition, I disliked people who talked about it around me. I felt, if I spoke that word, it was giving it too much power over me. In 1 John 4:4 it states, "Ye are of God, little children, and have overcome them; because greater is he that is in you, than he that is in the world" (KJV). I had to remember there was nothing more powerful than God. So I decided I was not going to let the enemy take possession of my mind and body. God does not give us the spirit of fear. I was not going to lay down and let this thing overtake me and ruin my life. I asked God to grant me peace. I was truly learning what faith was all about.

After receiving all the confirmations of the illness that had just changed my life, I had a choice to make. The doctors had laid the cards on the table and I had to make some major decisions regarding my health. I was told that the best route for me was to have a left breast mastectomy. I confided in my family and close friends that I trusted. I soon found out that not everyone is supportive in the most detrimental time in your life. Some individuals were negative, and I soon realized this was just another trick of the enemy to unsettle me. I prayed with my husband about my decision, and we decided it was best for me to have the surgery. I was so afraid what he would think of me once I had my breast removed. God knows our past, present and future. He knew just what man to place in my life. I remember my husband telling me that my life was what was important to him. He kiddingly said to me, it didn't matter if I had one, two or three breasts. Just as long as I was with him.

God truly granted me peace throughout this whole ordeal. There is no other way for me to explain it to you. I went through major surgery, had to take some time from work, but the blessings of God did not stop coming. For that period of time, I did not miss a paycheck and the bills were still paid. The presence of God overflowed my life. During my time of recuperation, I began to feel better and was able to do some outside activities with the help of some friends. I was currently a Girl Scout leader and decided to return to some of my meetings. I was refusing to let the enemy continue to disrupt my life. I was grateful for the help from family and Christian family members. This support added to my healing, spiritually, mentally and physically. I had started to feel more at peace with my situation, and was finally coming back to my old self. I knew that the enemy had lost this round and had left me alone. So I thought!! However, he had not. He came up with a fresh new batch of tarts to throw at me. One day, my husband had to stop off at my job to pick up my payroll check. During his visit, my coworkers gave him some get-well cards for me that they had collected. On his way home on the bus, he got off the bus and forgot my paycheck and the cards that he had laid in the seat next to him. So now, the enemy has decided to play hardball. He didn't know who he was messing with. I had decided to put my trust in God. I was tired of giving the enemy the power to whoop me. When my husband arrived home and told me what happened, we immediately went in prayer asking God to take control of the situation. Well, let me tell you! When we walk in the Master's will and trust in Him there should be nothing to fear. I had planned to call my job on that Monday to put a stop payment on my payroll check, and I figured that the get-well cards would just be a lost. However, God had already taken control of the situation! On that Saturday, while I was away from home, my husband stated that two young women came to the house looking for me. They had found my check and the cards on the bus. Again, the enemy had lost this round. Things will happen in our lives that we have no control over. There will be deaths, sicknesses, divorces, disobedient children and violence in the world. We just have to remember that we can be overcomers, not through our own strength, but through faith in God. He blessed the healing of my body and allowed me to return to work and the ministries at my church. I had decided I was going to be on fire for my Lord. He had blessed me with the victory of this round.

What I would like for us to remember is that we are not perfect. Often when God has blessed us with a victory, we promise Him that we would serve Him with all our heart until the day we die. And while that's our plan, we often get sidetracked somewhere down the road. God begins to take a back seat in our lives. He is no longer the driver. The wonderful thing about God is that He doesn't expect us to be perfect in this world. And I, too, was not perfect. I, too, would often allow myself to get sidetracked. But I knew it was only the trick of the enemy to get me to think I was all better now, and no longer needed to depend on God. That I was now "self-sufficient". I am so thankful for God's healing hand on me. He continued to bless me in abundance. In 2004, we bought our first new home and God allowed my husband to retire from work. I thought to myself, *God is protecting me now from any more turmoil in my life.* Surely, I had lost loved ones through the years that had saddened my heart, but God's comfort was there. The illness that had struck my body in 1998 was almost a blur in my mind. Only when I looked in the mirror at myself was I reminded of what I went through and how God granted me peace through that journey.

I realized that things would continue to happen in my life and often wondered if God was testing me. When I saw family members and loved ones become victim to cancer, I wanted to go into a closet and hide. I didn't want that disease to ever find me again, I just wanted to forget that this disease existed. I didn't want people to talk about cancer around me. I would turn the TV off if there were commercials advertising medical issues about cancer. When family and friends would mention it, I would think to myself, *how inconsiderate of them knowing what I have gone through*. Nevertheless, I now know I wasn't supposed to go and hide. I was going to be the poster child for God, telling others of my journey and my healing. Letting others know, **if He did it before, He could do it again**. I was not going to run from the enemy any longer. I was now the "Bad Mama Jama". I became an advocate for women with breast cancer. I did the yearly walks and the annual awareness events on my jobs. I was on a roll, and nothing was going to stop me or discourage me. My mind was focused and God was on my side. Nothing could stop me now. Or that's what I thought until it happened to a close family member. My grandson was afflicted with bone cancer. I thought, *no, this can't be, he is only seven years old*. I wanted answers and I wanted them now. Why was this happening to him? The enemy had entered my zone again and this time he wasn't playing. While helping to tend to my grandson's care, I had to take some time and have surgery to remove my gall bladder. I bounced back well from this surgery and moved on. Approximately four months after my surgery, I started to have some pain in my side. I went back and forth to the doctor and they told me it was just arthritis in my side. They gave me some pain medicine and blew me off. A couple weeks later, the pain became worse and was now on both sides. The doctor still said it was nothing. I want you to know that even in the midst of not being properly cared for by my doctor, I knew God was there. My body was telling me that something was wrong. One day, sitting at my desk, I experienced some bad chest pains. I decided to go to the Urgent Care facility, which sent me over to the emergency room. I had no idea that I was about to enter into the Storm of Storms in my life.

After several exams and tests, it was determined that the breast cancer had returned. Not only had it just returned, but it had returned with a vengeance; it had metastasized to other parts of my body. ARE YOU KIDDING ME? This cannot be happening, not again. I felt that the enemy had just thrown the entire box of tarts at me. Not only that, but he had turned the furnace up to 360 degrees. I was shocked, I was upset and I was pissed. Why is this happening? My mental control was off the chart. Here I am caring for my grandson and this happens. The family was already hurt and upset over his illness. How could I go tell them this? Why, God, why? I was so upset with my doctors, for seven months they had blown this off as arthritis allowing this thing to do major damage to my body. I was ready to file a lawsuit. Somebody was about to lose their license. This was unacceptable. I must have ranted and raved in my head for a couple of days.

After I calmed down, I remembered that the same God that was there in 1998 is the same one who is with me now. And *if He did it before, He can do it again!* I often think that God prepares us in small measures, allowing us to go through things to strengthen us for what He knows is ahead. Even though this time was much different and worse, my peace and calm was different. I asked God to give me some **PVH.** That was my daily note on my computer at work. Please bless me daily Lord with your PVH. **PEACE, VICTORY AND HEALING.** I had decided there wasn't going to be any pity party here, and the enemy might as well back off because I was ready to kick butt. I have always been known in my family as the one least likely to get into a fight. Nevertheless, I was ready for this battle. Well, I guess the enemy said bring it on, because a couple months later, my husband disclosed to me that he been diagnosed with prostate cancer in 2008 and did not tell me. The doctors had reassured him that it was under control and there was no need for him to worry, so he decided to keep it to himself. Unfortunately, his levels were starting to go up and the doctor was suggesting some treatment. Again, I felt the enemy was trying to tell me he was in control, but I knew who was. I went through some extensive surgery this time, having to have part of my right ribs removed because the cancer had damaged it so badly. But believe it or not, my leave time from work was shorter. But God!

Again, I went to God with my requests and concerns for my life. Sure, I was concerned about leaving my husband behind. Who would care for him? Who would help him? Everyone has their own family. I know now that God is our caretaker. He is the provider and He doesn't need our help to care for His people. I started reading some encouraging scriptures in the Bible, focusing on God and not my storm. I knew I was not alone on this journey.

One of my favorite scriptures is Mark 11:22-24; "Have faith in God," Jesus answered, "Truly I tell you, if anyone says to this mountain, Go, throw yourself into the sea." and does not doubt in their heart but believes that what they say will happen; it will be done for them. Therefore I tell you, whatever you ask for in prayer, believe that you have received it, and it will be yours" (KJV).

We don't have to lie down to the enemy when we are afflicted with troubles in our lives. We are more than conquerors; we are the children of the King. I encourage you to take hold and do some self-inventory of who you are. There is no way to stop the storms that will come in life. Many we will not have control over, but we do have control over how we react. If God blesses us to overcome one storm, He will be there for the next. As I said in the beginning, **If He did it before, He can do it again.**

"Now to Him who is able to do immeasurably more than all we ask or image, according to His power that is at work within us" (Ephesians 3:20, KJV).

Autograph Page

Mrs. Marian Steele

Transformation: From the Inside Out

About the Author
Mrs. Trease Sears

Trease Sears is a woman of God who believes that everything that happens in our lives has a purpose. It is up to us to determine how to use our tests, trials, tribulations and pain to bring forth healing for ourselves and others. She is a wife and mother; an author and mentor; a teacher and philanthropist. She wears a number of hats. She loves spending time with her family vacationing.

Trease's first book is called *The Art of Becoming One: A Spiritual Journey Toward Unity.* She is also the Executive Director of Sow One World Changes Summer Arts Program, held in Indiana.

Transformation: From the Inside Out

Acknowledgements

To my family and friends, immediate and extended, I love you all. Each of you holds a very special place in my heart. Thank you for being a part of my journey.

Transformation: From the Inside Out

Dedication

This work is dedicated to my dear husband. Thank you for seventeen years of marriage. I am grateful for the unconditional love that you have shown me throughout the years. There is no doubt in my mind that we were created for one another. I love you, baby.

Transformation: From the Inside Out

The Independent Married Woman

I don't need anyone to take care of me! I got this! I'm my own woman. Nobody can do it like I can. You can't tell me what to do. I had the power and everyone was going to know it.

I grew up not having a relationship with my biological father. My mother left him when I was four. Being a child, I had no control over what was happening in my life at that time. While I thought that this didn't have an effect on me, I later discovered that this actually had a major impact on the woman I was becoming. Even though God blessed me with the best stepfather on the planet, in my opinion, I still grew up dealing with low self-esteem. I didn't think I was good enough, pretty enough, or smart enough. I was always being teased about my teeth and my forehead. My hair was short and I was flat-chested. I would constantly compare myself to other girls my age. I hated to look in the mirror. I didn't think I was beautiful. Something had to be wrong with me, right? My father didn't want me. He never came for me. Although this wasn't something that I thought about every day, the seed of abandonment had taken root in my heart and soon began to sprout negative character traits that would have a lasting effect on my adult life. No matter how often I heard that I was beautiful and intelligent, my beliefs about myself were what I held on to. Until a person believes for themselves, it's difficult for change to take place.

Searching for love and acceptance, I was willing to allow just about anything. I had been lied to, talked about, cheated on and mistreated. Boys portraying men, whispering sweet nothings in my ears and that's exactly what they were talking about, NOTHING! However, my immaturity and the desire to be loved by a man overshadowed the reality that these relationships were not good for me. I was mistaking lust for love, trying to fill the void that abandonment had left behind. In the back of my mind, I knew that these relationships were not the best choices for me. It was almost as if I didn't care. I had control over my life now, or so I thought. I made my own decisions and didn't have to answer to anyone.

Transformation: From the Inside Out

There were times when the emptiness was overwhelming and unbearable. It was suffocating, yet I continued to engage in destructive behavior, all the while building a protective cage around my heart.

At sixteen, my boyfriend broke up with me. I did not want the relationship to end so I told him I was pregnant when really I wasn't. I went three months pretending to be pregnant until I realized that I would soon have to give birth. What was I going to do? After all, I could not produce a baby at the end of nine months. In my immature mind, there was only one thing left to do and that was to continue the lie by telling everyone that I had had a miscarriage. I felt bad; I couldn't believe what I had done, but that did not stop me from continuing with the lie. I was dying on the inside. I wanted to give up, but for some reason I couldn't.

Next thing I knew, I was seventeen and pregnant for real and on purpose. Somehow, in my mind, I thought having a baby would be the glue to hold my relationship together. My pregnancy was very stressful. At five months, it was discovered that my daughter had cysts on her brain and would have to have surgery immediately after birth. On January 14, 1994, my precious gift was born and I graduated high school one month before my eighteenth birthday. The month after my eighteenth birthday, I moved out of my parents' home. Everything was happening fast. I had this beautiful baby girl and she was depending on me. I could no longer live as though I wanted to give up.

Having a child with a severe disability caused me to grow up quickly. I had to make major decisions regarding my daughter's health and well-being. Her doctor said that she would not live to be two years old and if she did live past two, she would be confined to a wheelchair. It was my sole responsibility to care for her, but I would not allow myself to get too close to her for fear of losing her. At only two weeks old, she had her first surgery, and there were eight more by the time she was eighteen months old. I had to walk through the door of responsibility and "put on my big girl underwear." Nope, I was no longer a child. I had become independent, or at least I was exhibiting independent behaviors. My being grown had nothing to do with my age. The path I chose thrust me into adulthood. So-called friends told me that my life was over; some family members made me believe that my dreams would die from strangulation by the hand of my reality. I had to pay my own bills, handle my own business, work and take care of my child. At times, it was hard, sometimes even unbearable but I had to make it work in order to dispel the prophecies that had been spoken over my life.

At the age of twenty, I felt as if my life was missing something. I was tired of working dead-end jobs. It was time for me to embark upon my destiny and make something out of my life. Wanting to better myself and be a woman my daughter could be proud of, I enrolled in a local college. Raising my baby girl, working full-time and going to school proved to be a struggle, but I was determined to accomplish the goals that I had set. I had a full plate and a focused purpose and no time for love. I actually wasn't all that interested in love, anyway. I had to stay focused and in my past, the relationships that I participated in were more work than they were worth. Love never really worked out for me. After a few failed relationships and having to piece my broken heart together as best I could; I built a stone cage around it for protection. The exterior shell was callous and hard to cut through. No one would ever have access to my heart again. I was surface in everything I did. It was hard to get close to people because I didn't want to be disappointed. However, on the inside, I was dying a silent death. I wasn't able to live in or for the moment. I was always assessing every situation and every person's motives. I lived by the code, "guilty until proven innocent."

When I wasn't looking, I was found. I met my future husband. Just like me, he was on a path to bettering his life. He was funny, successful, giving and patient. Deep in my heart, I knew we were meant to be, but still, I was scared. Initially, our relationship was very surface, because I wouldn't allow him to be the answer of my heart's prayer. I lived in fear that history would repeat itself. Would he walk out and disappoint me like the others? After a year of

Transformation: From the Inside Out

dating, he asked me to be his wife. A few months before our wedding, we both re-dedicated our lives to Christ. As we were learning our new church home, how to be in relationship with our Heavenly Father and one another, the enemy was lurking in the shadows waiting for the opportune time to attack. We got married and moved into our new home and he pounced! It was like something took over me; my mind, body and spirit. There were days I was evil and hard to get along with for no reason at all. Looking back, I believe this was a defense mechanism, which I used to keep people from hurting and disappointing me. In my wrong thinking, I thought I was protecting myself. In reality, I was destroying my relationships. My husband only wanted to love me and he did just that. He loved me to my very core, rotten and all, even when I wasn't loving him back.

In my marriage, it was difficult for me to submit to my husband, not because of anything that he had or had not done. I was making him pay for the mistakes of past relationships. I continued to live my life as the independent, hurt woman I had become. I was making major decisions without consulting or even considering my husband's opinion. I was operating out of order. I had succumbed to the world's way of thinking. Selfishly seeking to meet my own needs, it was all about me. Cold and hard, my heart had no feeling. The insecurities that I carried as a child spilled over into my adult life. They affected my marriage and my other relationships, as well. I was so broken on the inside and I didn't even know it. My marriage suffered because of my brokenness. It was being sabotaged and I was the number one suspect.

I was cruel. Whenever we would have a disagreement, I would always revert to saying, "You can leave if you want to, and I will definitely be alright." The wall didn't allow me to completely give of myself, so if anyone walked out of my life, I made myself believe that it wouldn't phase me. In the back of my mind, I was waiting for the best relationship that I had ever had to come to an end. It was too good to be true. Who loves like this?

Transformation: From the Inside Out

God has put into place a special divine order when it comes to marriage (1 Corinthians 11:3). Not realizing that in a marriage we are responsible for submitting to one another, meeting one another's needs and praying for one another, I fulfilled my duties the best I knew how. Although, I was still learning, I was failing big time. I had become very active in ministry; there were often times that my home was neglected because I chose to be at church instead of with my family. In my mind, I thought the more I did for the Lord, the closer in relationship I could be with Him. This left me empty and lonely. I was leaving my family to fend for themselves, while I thought I was handling God's business; Sunday worship, dance rehearsal, Bible Study, Children's ministry and every other function held, I was there giving. Giving of myself until I was depleted. By the time I made it home, I had nothing to give; not to my husband or my children. As I took on these additional responsibilities, I unknowingly committed my husband to my plan. Someone had to be with the children, after all they couldn't care for themselves. I was selfish. I never considered his feelings. I knew the plans that I had for me, for my life and anything that didn't line up with those plans, I gave little to no attention. Due to my ignorance, I was operating outside of the will of God. I thank God for the women He allowed in my life; women who didn't have a problem telling me when I was wrong. Women who prayed with me and also for me in their private time with God. Women who were not ashamed of what it meant to be a daughter of the King. I can honestly say that these women helped me through some of my toughest times. They didn't give up, even when I wasn't willing to let them in.

Wives and mothers, let me encourage you. Home is your first ministry. If your home is not right, then that's where you should be. Making a difference in the lives of others, helping your church and being involved in your community are not bad, but they should not be done at the expense of your family. Be prayerful about the commitments that you make. Surround yourself with others who have a desire to please God; those who won't allow your foolishness to go unchecked.

After a while, my independence began to weigh me down. I was trying to be everything to everyone. Wanting to be accepted, all the while, not willing to open up and let anyone in. My heart was hard as stone. It was as if the very life was being sucked out of me. It literally hurt to take deep breaths. My heart was racked with pain and I had allowed it.

My marriage, my relationship with my children, and my relationship with God were all surface. These were the people closest to me. They were the people who mattered the most. I was going through the motions. I knew what to say and when to say it but deep down my plan was to protect myself by any means necessary. I was in a house full of people and yet I felt so alone. I hadn't done what was necessary to build relationships with my husband or my children. In hindsight, I wrapped myself in ministry work as a protective measure. I had psyched myself into believing that if something were too happened to them, I wouldn't feel the pain. That seed of abandonment planted so long ago had now begun to take on a life-threatening form. I had to make some changes, but how?

As I began to grow in my relationship with God, I grew a strong desire to please Him. I wanted to trust Him more, but because of past disappointments and trust issues it was difficult to allow Him into my heart. I wouldn't let go of all that I had been through. I felt that if I let my guard down and something happened, it would be my fault. My past had an exceedingly tight grip on my future. I couldn't shake it, and I desperately wanted to. My plans for my life were smothering me. There had to be a better way. What was I doing? I had missed out, on so much. After many tears, I began to read the Word daily. However, it was hard for me to accept the fact that God loved me. I wasn't worthy of a love like His. What about the things that I had done? Or what about the people I had hurt while I was so-called protecting myself? He couldn't possibly love me the way that His Word described. Contrary to what

Transformation: From the Inside Out

I believed, when I reflect on my past, it was evident that He was there loving me every step of the way.

One day in self-reflection, I remember asking the Lord to take my heart of stone and give me a heart of flesh. At the time, I was not aware that this was an actual scripture (Ezekiel 36:26). Yet, He began to do just that. I could feel Him chipping away at the stone cage I had built around my heart so many years ago. I no longer had to live life in bondage. I could take deep breaths and not feel as though I was having a heart attack.

Through the study of His Word, I learned about the sacrifice He made so that I could be here, so that I could live a life of freedom. The more I studied His Word and opened up to Him about my deepest fears, failures, hurts, and desires; healing began to take place. He was healing me from the inside out. There were no judgments. I could feel His love. I was no longer that four-year-old little girl with no control. Once I was able to truly receive God's love for me, I was set up to open my heart and accept the love of my husband, my children and others. I began to share my heart with them and my relationships began to blossom. I was now experiencing true love, in its purest form, and that was just what my heart needed. I wouldn't get back the years I had missed but this new, fresh start was the beginning of something more beautiful than I could have ever imagined.

It hurts my heart to know that I didn't exhibit to my husband the love that he desired from me, and yet he continued to love me unconditionally. He was very patient with me. I know that he was secretly praying for my deliverance, as a husband should do. He has forgiven me and we are able to move forward. The enemy would have liked for me to beat myself up and get tangled in his devastating web of defeat. There are times when I do get stuck there, but God gives me a gentle nudge to move it along. He won't allow me to dwell on my past mistakes. There is too much work to be done for the Kingdom. My husband and I share our story with other married couples and those soon to be married. God has blessed us with multiple opportunities to help others avoid the snares and traps that we had to endure.

My unchecked internal issues caused a lot of unnecessary stress and strain on my marriage and other relationships, but I bless God for restoration. After seven years of marriage and growing in my relationship with God, He began to show me myself. At times, this was hard to deal with, because I thought I had it all together. I didn't realize the damage I was causing to the ones I claimed to love. My heart hurt, but now for a different reason. I had to make some changes. It has not been an easy journey, but we are taking it day by day.

No matter what issues you have faced in your marriage up to this point, know that marital joy is obtainable. There is nothing too hard for God. You have tried everything and everyone else, why not try Him? Now, I'm not saying He is going fix it but He has a way of removing the scales from your eyes so that you can see it from a different perspective.

For those reading who are not married, take heed, resolve your past issues before you walk down the aisle. Gain understanding of God's divine order and operate in it. If you want your union to last and be blessed do your part to make it happen.

Autograph Page

Mrs. Trease Sears

Transformation: From the Inside Out

About the Author

Minister Schurronda White

Minister Schurronda White was born and raised in Indianapolis, Indiana.

Minster White attends Freewill Christian Ministries Church, where she loves serving God and His people. Minister White teaches Sunday school, is a part of the Hospitality Ministry, teaches New Members class, and is over the Pastors Partners Ministry.

Her favorite Bible passage is Romans, Chapter 8.

In Minister White's spare time she volunteers at the church daycare, where she is affectionately known as "Mother" White. She enjoys reading and spending time with family and friends.

Minister White has worked in the telecommunications industry for a total of forty years.

Minister White is the proud mother of a daughter, Minister Melissa Lewis, and grandmother to three grandchildren: Brien, Destiny and James.

Acknowledgements

To God Almighty, all honor and glory for who You are. Without You, I am nothing.

To my Pastors, Eddie and Notoshia Howard: thank you for being the shepherds after God's own heart. Thank you for loving, supporting, encouraging and equipping me.

To my daughter, grandchildren, and family: I thank God. He has blessed me to have you. Thank you for your love and support.

Transformation: From the Inside Out

Transformation: From the Inside Out

Stepping Out

I was born a middle child. I remember feeling ignored, alone, left out, and not fitting in. I have an older sister, and a younger sister who was born early. For four days of the year we are the same age. Mother told me she thought that I would take her bottle. My younger sister was sickly, so she got a lot of attention. Five years later, my brother was born. Up until this point, my parents had three girls; so it was natural for my mother to pack girls clothes to bring my brother home. I was bashful and I was shy. I was not a talker. I listened more than I talked.

I did not like who I was or how I looked. I wanted to be someone else; like a Barbie doll, be pretty, thin, smart, have many friends, and have all kinds of clothes, shoes, and purses. I thought that would make me perfect. I thought if I were like Barbie, everyone would like me. I would fit in, because everyone loves Barbie!

There is something about every one of us that we do not like. I wanted to be everyone's friend.

I did not want anyone to be mad at me. I wanted to get along with everyone, so I would not express how I truly felt. I would hold it in. Middle children are compromisers.

I would compromise to get along in order to fit in. I wanted to be a team player. Instead of expressing myself, I would swallow it and put everyone else's feelings first. I would stay out of everyone's way. What everyone else wanted is what I would settle for and it became what I wanted.

I was quiet, introverted, and shy. I only spoke when I was spoken to. In school, teachers would put on my report card, "She needs to speak up more in class." I enjoyed history class and English, and I was considered a nerd. My younger sister was the cheerleader and the popular one at school. People would refer to me as "Pam's sister", and did not even know my name. I associated myself with other nerds like me, and I was a member of the history club. I never wanted to be the center of attention. I have always been in the background. I never had to be seen or heard in school. I was invisible. I did not talk in class, and I did my work, but I never expressed myself.

Food was my escape. Food was comforting to me. If I had an issue and I could not talk about it, I would eat. I would eat to feel better. I would eat because I was mad. I would eat when I could not express how I felt. I would eat when I was picked on. Food always made me feel better. Food is how I chose to vent my frustrations. If I felt threatened and did not want to make anyone mad, I would eat to forget about it. Food did not hurt any body's feelings; food was everything to me.

I did not like the way I looked. I wanted to lose weight. I did not look like the average young woman. I started taking diet pills, because I thought that was the answer to lose weight quickly. I consumed so much caffeine that I could not sleep for days, my heart would race and I would be so hyper, but I did not eat. I found out that diet pills contained a substance that could cause death. I decided I would go on a diet, but that would turn into extreme dieting. Eating once a day worked until I started eating normally again. I thought if I eat once a day to lose weight, I could look like Barbie. I would lose weight, and then gain it right back, I would yo-yo diet, and it did not work. At the time, I did not realize I needed to work on the inside of me before I would ever be satisfied with the outside.

What we think and feel about ourselves affects every part of our lives. What I feel about myself affects my relationships with family and friends. What I feel about myself also affects my confidence, which in turn affected my choices in life. What I feel about myself will affect my destiny in life.

When we like ourselves, we are content with our choices. When we like ourselves, we make better choices. When we know who we are, we can walk in our destiny.

What we feel about ourselves affects our marriages. I heard someone tell their spouse, "Your job is to make me happy." True happiness does not come from someone else. Happiness comes

Transformation: From the Inside Out

from the inside. No one can force us to like the skin we are in. No one can force us to have confidence in the way we are. There is emptiness when I do not know who I am. How can I be happy if I do not like the skin I am in?

I was raised as a Christian. My mother was a churchgoer, and we went to church all of our childhood. I know who God is; I know He is the Creator of everything. I know that Jesus died so we could have eternal life.

It took me going through major sickness with my mother for me to realize who I truly am. I learned that God is able to walk with us every day; giving us love, encouragement, strength and courage.

I remember being in the room when the doctor told my mother, she had breast cancer, and that the lump was the size of a grapefruit. I could not believe it, I did not understand. I heard a voice next to me saying, "Would it be okay if I pray for you?" It was the hospital chaplain. I was scared, and I was alone because my husband was working in another state at the time. My siblings lived in another state. My father was very upset, and I did not know how to comfort him. I was thinking, *what am I going to do? How can I fix this?* I was trying to figure how what I needed to do to keep everything normal. When the chaplain prayed, he helped me to realize I had a God who loved me, and who was there to help me; a God who would not leave me or forsake me. I would pray before, but I thought I could handle all of my issues. I did not truly give my problems to God to handle. I thought I was in charge and that I could fix my own issues. I realized I could not handle this issue on my own. I talked with and prayed to God. God is faithful. My Mother got the lump removed, and she did not have to have any kind of cancer treatment. My mother lived a long time as a cancer survivor.

God is the Almighty, and He can do anything but fail. God showed me through my prayers that He loves me and that I am important to Him. My issues and problems mattered to Him. God heard my prayers and He answered right on time. During this time, God brought my sister back home to be there, for me, and my mother. My mother had other health challenges, but God saw her through them all. In the process, I saw strength through the sickness my mother had. I saw how God was right there with us through every situation. I saw how God uses His faithful servants to be examples of His divine healing. God showed me that He hears our cries for help. God is faithful and He keeps His promises.

I saw that God was there for my mother, and that God was working things out in me through her sickness. I learned how to pray and to trust God, as well as how to wait on God. I learned how to lean and depend on God to solve any issue. I learned that God wants to answer our prayers. I learned how I can pray and go to God anytime, and He is always listening. I did not feel ignored, nor did I feel invisible. I could pray and tell God all about my troubles. I learned that God loves me and wants the best for me. I learned how to step out on faith.

At my job, there was an opening to become a trainer. I applied for the job. Originally, I had talked myself out of the position. *They are never going to pick me. I have never done training before. I am an introvert. I don't look like the other trainers. I am not qualified.* I went ahead and submitted the request for the job with my boss anyway. I was interviewed by my boss who mentioned you can teach about the products, but you cannot teach people skills. I had experience in training. I had taught Sunday school for a long time. I prayed and asked God to bless me. God blessed me, and I got the job. Now the fun begins. I had to travel to customer sites and do customer training. The first customer I went to, I was so nervous and unsure of myself that I was physically ill. It was God who gave me the courage to stand in front of people who I did not know. It was God who gave me the courage to travel across the state. One time, I lost my directions to the customer site; they had flown out of the car window. This was before we had smartphones and GPS.

I asked God to take the wheel. God got me to all of the destinations and back safely. I prayed before I opened my mouth. I remember not being able to talk when I got excited and nervous. I prayed for God to lead and guide me. To go from a kid who could

Transformation: From the Inside Out

not even look at people when I talked to them, to standing in front of people training them, I had stepped out on faith. God worked out any nervousness I had. I never got a customer complaint or had any issues when I traveled. I was nominated for the trainer of the year and won. I received numerous customer compliments. I give the glory to God.

I currently handle the telecommunications system for a private college with 140 sites. If there are any issues with the phone system, it is my responsibility to identify the issue and get the issue resolved. Many times, I have issues that no one can figure out. I pray to God to reveal to me the issue. Many times, God provided the resolution. With God all things are possible!

I have always enjoyed working and serving in church. I have always been on the hospitality committee, usher board and the nursing staff. I enjoy washing dishes. I was just content serving in the background, never wanted to be out front. Never needed to stand in front of people, or someone, who needed to be seen by others. I am good at helping others stand out and helping others lead. I consider myself a great supporter. A good helper: that is how I would describe my church work. Someone has to serve the leaders, and that has always been me. One day, I was working in the kitchen at church. I was told that it was time for me to come out of the kitchen, and come out of the background. I was told the same thing by three different people of God, which I was called to preach the word of God. I immediately thought *who me?* I am not an out-front person. I do not want any attention drawn to me. I am too quiet and I am not educated, so I thought they were mistaken. I asked God, "Do you really want me?" I talked myself into not being qualified. There were plenty of other people who would jump at the chance to be out front. I took a long time to ponder over the decision to accept my calling into ministry. I told myself that I will continue to do what I was doing; working in the background and teaching Sunday school.

As part of our spiritual training, we were asked to take a spiritual gift test. I thought I knew my spiritual gifts; I am compassionate, I am a teacher, and I am a giver. I took the test and the results were different from what I thought to be my spiritual gifts. The test said that I was a Pastor. I could not believe it! I wanted to take the test again. I figured there was no way, could I be a Pastor. I am not a leader, and I am a worker. I prayed for clarity. I constantly questioned my calling.

I was teaching Sunday school one day, and the subject was about being chosen by God. As I taught, I received revelation that God chooses whom He wants. God chose David, the youngest and the weakest of all the brothers. God looks at our hearts, not what's on the outside. God does not see what others see. God does not measure us by worldly standards. God chooses our spiritual gifts according to His will. I learned that if God has called you, He will equip you. I learned God does not need me. I learned it is a privilege to be chosen by God. God has a given purpose for all of our lives. I embraced the call that God has placed on my life. I embraced the elevation God has called me to. Stepping out on faith is what God has asked me to do. It is not about me, it is about God and the power He has put in me. I chose to stop talking about what I am not, and start talking about who God is. Stop operating in "I am not good enough", "I am not smart enough", "I am not educated enough". However, I am who God says that I am.

I consider myself a cheerful giver. If someone is in need, I try to help in any way that I can. That is one of my spiritual gifts, I agree with. I enjoy giving to others. I would do without to give to others. Along with other areas of our lives, we have to give our finances, to God. First, we must understand that tithes are for our benefit and not God's. God does not need our money. Tithing is to teach us financial discipline. God knows exactly what He is doing. I am a tither. Matthew 6:33 states, "But seek first his kingdom and his righteousness, and all these things will be given to you as well" (NIV).

God also expects us to be good stewards with what He has blessed us with financially. I am constantly giving and giving. Did you not think to ask God who He wants you to sow into? What would be good ground to sow into? We have not because we ask not. I got so deep into debt that I had to file bankruptcy. I did not want to do it. Filing bankruptcy, to me, meant I was a failure. I could not take care of my business.

Yes, I mismanaged my finances. Yes, I did it all by myself. I did not ask God who and what to sow into, and I made financial decisions without consulting Him. I even consulted Wealth Management Company. When the planes hit the World Trade Center, the stock market crumbled. I lost most of my investments. If I would have asked God and listened to His financial planning, I could have avoided financial bankruptcy.

For five years, I had to submit to the bankruptcy judge and make payments to my debtors. God never left me, He was right there with me. God showed me the difference between a need and a want. God has even changed my wants. I realized a lot of things we think we want, we do not need. There was never a day when I was hungry or cold. I always had a roof over my head. I learned to ask God for advice and wait for God to answer. I learned to have patience, and not to make rash decisions. God has cattle on a thousand hills, and He knows what is best.

God made ways out of no ways financially, for me. When I did not see the way to pay my bills, God provided a way. I learned that paying my tithes gives God permission to handle my business. He is the best financial planner we could ever have. God knows the future and He knows how to plan ahead. I have learned to step out and trust God with my finances.

Once I surrendered my will to God, and recognized the plans that He has for my life, I received peace. It does not matter how old we are. God does not care about our natural age. God is a restorer of strength and health. It is all about walking in our God given destiny. God began to show me that He picked me for a reason. It is not about me but what God wants to do thru me. God knows exactly whom I can reach. God does not always give us the whole picture. I think if He showed me everything, I would want to run away. God knows just how much we can take at one time.

Transformation: From the Inside Out

    I have learned we are created in God's image. God loves us beyond measure. Everyone is important to God. God has awesome plans for our lives. We will make mistakes. No matter the circumstance, God is there for us. We have to step out on faith, and know that God will complete the work He has begun in us.

Autograph Page

Minister Schurronda White

Transformation: From the Inside Out

About the Author

Ms. Roberta Lynn Williams-Bell

Roberta Lynn Williams-Bell has provided community services for the past twenty-seven years in the capacity of: Behavioral Rehabilitation Specialist, Case-Manager, Head Start Teacher, Substance Abuse Counselor and Therapist. Roberta holds a Bachelor's of Science Degree specializing in Family Studies and Gerontology, as well as a Master's of Business Administration degree. During obtaining both degrees, she was a devoted single parent of Sedrick, Herbert, Ciera and Tyrique. Roberta is dedicated to continue to start and grow relationships with the individuals that God brings into her life. "Being confident of this, that he who began a good work in you will carry it on to completion" (Philippians 1:6 NIV).

Transformation: From the Inside Out

Acknowledgements

To all of my family and friends from the community of Chickasha, Oklahoma: thank you for all your love and support.

To God be the Glory!

Transformation: From the Inside Out

Transformation: From the Inside Out

A Love Story

As humans, we have a strong sense and need to be loved. Humans take a lot of pride in families. The family is usually a person's first teacher about the world around them. Animals do not have the same need as humans to be needed and loved. It is the need for love in our lives and to be connected with others that evolves into developing lifetime relationships.

Our relationships with others are also what is referred to as "socialization". Socialization norms are set by the society into which a human is born in. The values of the family are reflected in society. It takes something concrete for the human to connect to in order to feel as though they are loved and as if their lives have meaning.

To me, love means long-term, unconditional caring and obligation. Love is priceless, and yet there is not enough of it in the world. Trust, loyalty, ethics, responsibility, and compromise are all important factors in the cornerstones of building a family. A family cannot function as a unit unless there is love, loyalty, responsibility and flexibility among one another. Each of these characteristics have to be consistently instilled and reinforced with good communication.

My life began when a sixteen, year old high school gave birth to me in Chickasha, Oklahoma. It is a small town with a population of around 16,000. In the grey winter month of November, I became a sixteen-year-old, African-American, high school dropout and runaway. At birth, my life was already facing unbelievable odds! My grandmother would often share her story of fighting with the state authority to release her daughter from the state girls' home, to find out that her daughter was also in her initial trimester of pregnancy. She would add to the story with how she had confided in the local authority to alert them of her concern for her runaway daughter, but not feeling as though she deserved to be put in a state girls' school as punishment.

At birth, life presented several obstacles. But God had already considered such a unique plan and unconditional act of love. The first most unique act of love was bestowed upon me when my biological mother unselfishly presented me to her parents, my grandparents, to rear me as their daughter. Immediately, that made my life different because my grandparents raised me as their youngest daughter of their five children. This arrangement made my birth mother the oldest sister. The eldest son was eighteen, middle son was seventeen, and next to youngest daughter was nine. This was the trend of the era for grandparents to raise their grandchildren.

    How unselfish was it for Doretha and Willie to accept the responsibility of an infant whom they were unsure of the beginning and ending of? Where I would be if it were not for them accepting this divine assignment of rearing me? The total problem and solution is one that considers major soul searching. A teenage mother whom cannot provide for their child emotionally, financially mentally or physically. What are the options of such situations?

    At an early age, my parents allowed the exploration and curiosity of my surroundings. I was doted on by my parents. Nature and nurture were provided daily in the home. The memories of living in a rural community, knowing all of my neighbors. At such young age, visiting them or going to the farm to feed the animals, I had a simple but peaceful life. In the family yard there were peach, plum and apple trees, along with blackberry vines. Every summer, my mother would chase the children of the neighborhood off her fruit trees. My older siblings would spend time as caregivers, at times. I can remember the music that was played by my brothers and my sister keeping me in the latest fashion. For ten years of my childhood, I had regular scares with asthma, which made the attention that was provided by my parents more intense. Most of my time was spent with my mother, a full-time homemaker. I remember the fear I had each time I was admitted to the hospital, which was twice a year, once in the spring and once in the fall. My older siblings would become jealous at times because of the attention and time my parents would provide to me.

Transformation: From the Inside Out

At the age of four, I entered into public school. This was overwhelming because of the commitment it required to stay there for up to six hours. Actually interacting with other children that were my age, it was overwhelming! Due to the dependence I had on the support of my blanket and my bottle. Everyday upon getting off of the school bus at home, I would recover my bottle that was hidden in my special place from my mother, and fill it with syrup and corn syrup, then drink up! During these early years, I learned the benefits of friendships and relationships. At that very age, I learned that everything we do is based on relationships. The relationships within our community, family and within the world we live in are extremely important.

In the seventies, life was good for a middle-class family in American. Relationships were strong among communities and families, with the support of church and schools. Fibers of the community were tightly woven in this small, rural community. Our community promoted a sense of unity. Each family had a story, and everyone knew this story. At a young age, you learned that bad news grows like a wildfire!

At the age of five, I had the opportunity to join the Brownie troop at my school. The education and enjoyment that was gained from the relationships that this experience gave me one of several initial influences and character builders. The interactions provided social etiquette training, along with the experience of building relationships with other girls from different cultures. At this age, my engagement in participating independently in church activities began, as well. Both of these organizations had one thing in common; honor to GOD! I gained experiences and relationships that I benefited from and that lasted from decade to decade.

As time evolved, I began to move into my pre-teenage years, struggling with my body, identity and position in this big world. Although there was nothing I lacked and was always groomed in the very best attire by my parents, the relationships with my peers were challenging. Often, I would get cornered or bullied by the other children due to jealousy. Eventually, I was engaging in verbal or physical fights with peers almost weekly. Often leaving a fight not knowing what the fight was even about. To this day, in my adulthood, I am not able to understand the animosity the female gender allows to grow inside them based on little to no truths. How quick we are as group to put one another down according to shallow pretenses!

In my teenage years, I struggled with accepting authority. I began to sell marijuana, party at nightclubs, and just about everything else, I could get away with at the age of fifteen. The foundation that my parents established within me as a youth had begun to crack. This was the beginning of taking advantage of the fact that my parents never felt a need to discipline me and would certainly not allow others to do so.

At age fifteen, I was pregnant. At age sixteen, I gave birth to my first son. I was a teenage parent. This was the first time in my life that I had feelings of embarrassment and shame. I was overwhelmed with the unknown future of my unborn child and myself. A lot happened during the pregnancy. Withdrawal from school because it was not appropriate for an unwed, teen to attend high school in the community I resided in. I was an outcast! Of course, the father of my unborn infant had decided that he would not engage in this quick transformation from childhood to adulthood. The truth is, most likely if the physical changes were not actually taking place with my body, I would have dealt with this life-changing event through denial. It just so happened to be that this creation was actually growing and living within my vessel; a daily reminder that life is always evolving.

God is the originator of the family arrangement. Parenthood was a big step for a teenager! Upon birth of my infant, despite all of the heartache felt throughout the nine months after inception, I felt an urgency to be responsible due to the beauty and love God had bestowed on me! It was love at first sight! This was the actual first time in my life that God had showed his great character, strength and love to me! My thought was, *I need to know more about this God! One that can author creation in such a way!* As parents, seeds are planted. As parents, we will reap the harvest that we sow into our children. As a parent, I attempted to implant love and obedience to God to my children.

Instantly, a desire to recreate the simple and happy images my grandparents had allowed me to experience as a child were exactly what I desired for my own son. I thought, *Wow! I have my own family!* Suddenly, the disadvantages of being a teenage mother were present. I did not have the experience of life, nor the establishment of resources it took to live daily and most importantly, to meet the obligations of caring for another individual. Within the following two years after the birth of my son, completion of a high school education and to enroll in college were my primary goals.

I experienced anger, pain, and frustration with the relationship between my biological mother and myself. I was hurt to learn that the relationship I had established with my real mother was all a lie; despite the fact that my (grand) parents hadn't treated me as anything less than royalty. No matter how beautiful, how well-behaved, or how intelligent I was; I never obtained an honest relationship with my actual mother. In reminiscing, I think back to a time in my life that my biological mother would not even welcome me to her home, as if I were a stranger. All the thoughts of not being good enough were birthed in my subconscious mind, yet again. What could cause such disconnect between a child and parent?

When I first became a parent, the initial thought I had was to be the best parent I could be! A parent that would weather through a storm with my children, no matter what the outcome would be. I asked God to make a covenant with me to ensure that I would be able to raise my children. I was on a true quest for the knowledge I needed to be a good parent. I often referred back to the advice of a past educator who would quote regularly, "there is no excuse for ignorance."

At the age of eighteen, I was married. How unprepared I was for this major act of being a mother and wife! It felt as if I actually jumped from the pot to the frying pan. My primary trainer for this role was my mother, whom was actually my grandmother and the matriarch of our family. Initially, I thought that my role was to be a home-maker, which would consist of spending my days cooking, cleaning, sewing and shopping for my family. Needless to say, life did not work out that way. I was a working mother! I can remember relating to the song "I'm Every Woman". My husband struggled with an addiction, which caused a major strain on our relationship.

This small-town girl instantly got a reality check. The responsibility of the family was upon me, literally. My husband's addiction spiraled out of control, which led to domestic violence. Weekly, the fights got more intense due to his drinking, drugging and violent outbursts. The police had to be called several times. Family life was stressful! How could I have made such a poor choice? I was certainly confused about the four letter word 'love'. I loved my husband and knew him before the illness of addiction had overtaken him. Sometimes I wanted my marriage, and other times I was living in fear because of it. I knew a decision would have to be made; one that was too big to even wrap my thoughts around.

The day before my father succumbed to his death, following a seven-year battle with cancer, he requested that I come and sit with him in his room. At that time, he stated, "I am leaving and want you to let your husband fly away. With him, you will never have peace. So, promise me you will." The following summer after my grandfather's death, God gave me a mustard seed of courage to make a final attempt to remove my children and myself out of that volatile relationship. I did just as my father had requested. It was not easy, because this instantly changed my identity, social status and role.

Abruptly, I was a single mother of four children! I was totally confused, because this is not how I thought life was supposed to be for me. I was supposed to have the children and live in the white house with the white picket fence, just as my grandparents had. I had to be the mother, father, and bread winner all-in-one. My extended family was our support. The appreciation I have for extended family that shared support to my family during this time is immeasurable. My parents', again, displayed the unconditional love they had. They provided emotional, financial, and mental support to my new family. In reflection, I do not know what I would have done without such love throughout that time in my life.

God would not have created a beautiful family unit without also making provisions for their well-being. That is not God's character! The greatest happiness in my family was the birth of my children. Each of them were born naturally, with no complications. At each birth, it was love at first sight. Wow, God really loves me to shower me with such blessings.

My family attended church regularly. As long as God is first, everything else will be okay. It was essential to teach my children the importance of prayer. Single parenthood required a closer walk with God for our family's everyday necessities. Living a life of faith is the only way the family will truly have happiness. A family without God's wisdom and guidance are lost in today's world. They are confused when facing day-to-day trials in the world. A family who does not worship God together may struggle with an initial foundation and ultimate goal in life.

Honestly, sometimes I would catch myself just looking up at the sky and asking God for direction and understanding as a single parent. I suggest that each individual find scriptures and songs to keep in their heart and mind attuned to the Love of God, to assist with staying encouraged through their most trying times. I am sharing a couple that have kept me encouraged through the most discouraging of times.

My Life Song

Source: His Eye Is on the Sparrow
Civilla D. Martin, 1905

My Life Scripture of Significant

Matthew 10:29-31

"Are not two sparrows sold for a farthing? and one of them shall not fall on the ground without your Father. But the very hairs of your head are all numbered. Fear ye not therefore, ye are of more value than many sparrows"

My Life's Foundational Scripture

Psalms 139

"O lord, thou hast searched me, and known me. Thou knowest my downsitting and mine uprising, thou understandest my thought afar off. Thou compassest my path and my lying down, and art acquainted with all my ways. For there is not a word in my tongue, but, lo, O Lord, thou knowest it altogether. Thou hast beset me behind and before, and laid thine hand upon me. Such knowledge is too wonderful for me; it is high, I cannot attain unto it. Whither shall I go from thy spirit? or whither shall I flee from thy presence? If I ascend up into heaven, thou art there: if I make my bed in hell, behold, thou art there. If I take the wings of the morning, and dwell in the uttermost parts of the sea; Even there shall thy hand lead me, and thy right hand shall hold me. If I say, Surely the darkness shall cover me; even the night shall be light about me. Yea, the darkness hideth not from thee; but the night shineth as the day: the darkness and the light are both alike to thee. How precious also are thy thoughts unto me, O God! how great is the sum of them! If I should count them, they are more in number than the sand: when I awake, I am still with thee. Surely thou wilt slay the wicked, O God: depart from me therefore, ye bloody men. For they speak against thee wickedly, and thine enemies take thy name in vain. Do not I hate them, O Lord, that hate thee? and am not I grieved with those that rise up against thee? I hate them with perfect hatred: I count them mine enemies. Search me, O God, and know my heart: try me, and know my thoughts: And see if there be any wicked way in me, and lead me in the way everlasting" (KJV).

My character of women from the Bible is one of Esther; as a youth, I was dependent on the direction of my uncles and aunts. As an adult, I have sat among Kings of foreign lands and Ambassadors of my own land, none of them knowing my story of; abandonment, anger, domestic-violence, drug selling and teen-age pregnancy. The truth is through redemption I discovered the truth about Love (Corinthians 13) and the revelation that God as my father (Psalms 27).

My story is for those who are bound by all of life situations and have struggled with negative thoughts! My prayer is that my testimony will assist individuals with the courage to walk in the design that God has ordained for their life! It is by his grace that we are saved (Ephesians, 2:8).

Grace is given to us for our sins. He loves us anyway. Justification is something we need to justify our place in this world. Sanctification is the authority God has provided over our spiritual being. Assurance is what He gives us through love.

Most recently, God had ordered my steps to provide services in an adolescent girls' mental health residential hospital as a Mental Health Specialist; a modern-day girls' reformatory. The irony is that my mother was in a state reformatory during her first trimester of pregnancy with me. As a professional, I could not help but wonder, *which of these young ladies' personal situation fit or is the same as my biological mother's*? Walking the halls of the facility daily, I would say to myself *life is indeed a complete circle*!

One day, while I was at work, my sister called and told me she was at a doctor's visit. During this call, my sister stated that the doctor had delivered the news that she was in stage four of breast cancer and that the cancer had spread into her bones. I was speechless! Before I could say anything, I heard her say, "Bob, it is over!" I was hurt and unable to move as she ended the conversation and the phone line went dead. I attempted to put myself back together in order to continue my shift. Quickly transitioning into prayer while I was walking around the building. My mind and heart felt as though they had been attacked by a sharp weapon. My sister was only thirty-eight years old! I requested that God have mercy on us. The sting of death has been felt by our family three times within this decade alone; my two brothers (uncles) and sister (aunt).

At this time, I began to cry out to God. I asked Him, first, for His will in our life and begged Him for mercy! Shortly after this heartbreaking news, I traveled from Indianapolis to Oklahoma City to visit my sister. During the drive, there was a feeling of disbelief. I practiced self-talk to assist with regulating my emotions. During the visit, the air was tense with depression and despair. We fellowshipped and prayed together. Each member that was present had a lot say, but none of us had the courage to speak about this tragedy that we were forced to helplessly witness.

After I returned to Indianapolis, my sister called me and stated that she had gone into the hospital and underwent some treatment. I was hopeful, but in her voice I could hear the pain as she spoke with such pushed speech. She stated, "I did not choose this disease and I am going to try to fight to be here longer with my five children!" I was proud of her, because I have never heard my sister speak with such clarity or authority in my life. Again, I was speechless!

As time went on, I made several visits from Indiana to Oklahoma in attempt to get closer to my sister. This sister was my actual sister, as she was the daughter of my biological mother. They had the daughter and mother relationship together, and I envied this. Even so, she was still my baby sister, and was always one that I had taken up under my wing throughout life. Our relationship was one of love and hate, due to our age difference and being reared in different homes.

During one trip to visit my sister in Oklahoma City, as I was getting settled into my living quarters, my cell phone was bombarded with phone calls. I thought that it was just my family anticipating my visit, but actually, they were delivering the news that three of my younger family members had been shot in an apartment by an unknown shooter. My family knows that I am a prayer warrior! Glory be to God, they all survived their injuries. "The thief cometh not, but for to steal, and to kill, and to destroy." (John 10:10)

Transformation: From the Inside Out

During the visit to my sister's home, I laid across my sister's bed and mustered up the courage to ask her the one question that had been in the back of my mind. I began with an apology and followed with the most selfish question in the world: "What do you want me to think of, if you were to leave?" I went on to say, "I know you will cross my mind and I will miss you!" She stated "just think of love!"

My sister was not much of a traveler, but requested to go on vacation with me and my family! How excited we were for her to join us this vacation. Right away, we began to plan a trip to Miami, as well as a cruise! We all flew into Florida from our different locations; my daughter from Dallas, and my mother, sister, son and adoptive daughter from Oklahoma. The date our vacation started was on Mother's Day, 2015. How perfect and what a blessing it was to see my sister at the beach and smiling! I felt the same joy I had felt as a seven-year-old who was seeing my baby sister for the very first time. During the trip, I pushed my sister through the streets of Nassau and throughout the canvas of the City of Atlantis Resort in her wheelchair. We talked to each other, rather than talking at each other; quality time that I will cherish always.

Shortly after our trip in May, the phone calls began to be few and far between. The last text from my sister read, "Finally close my eyes again. I just want to let you know even though we did not always see eye to eye, I always knew I could come running to you and I knew that you would be in my corner; the good, bad and ugly. This is all that matters to me. Love, your sis Tish." In August, I had a dream of my sister dancing, prancing across a field like a gazelle. This dream was telling me that there was a spiritual transformation going on within my sister, because I knew my sister was unable to walk because of the cancer in her bones. It was time for me to head home to share my sister's destiny.

Upon driving into Oklahoma City, my daughter called my biological mother and stated that we needed to come to the hospital because my sister's health had dramatically declined. Upon arrival to the emergency room, my sister held out her hands and I asked her, "Did you wait on me?" She replied, "Yes." As the nurse was taking her for a CAT scan, I asked her, "Do you take on Jesus as you Lord and Savior? Do you believe that He rose from death?" Again, she said "Yes." I was happy, because I knew that God will provide for my sister at this time of darkness and for certain will be seeing my sister again.

    My sister passed within a year of her initial diagnosis of cancer. It had spread throughout her body and eventually into her brain. What a tragedy! I felt helpless, having to just sit and watch her deteriorate. The night she passed, her five children, my biological mother and I were at her home. In reminiscence, the activities of that night were carried on; cleaning, cooking and watching television. All attempts at trying to avoid that my sister was indeed passing away. Out of all of the places in the world, I was able to be with my sister and I'm thankful to God for that opportunity!

    I am convinced that nothing can ever separate us from God's love. Neither death nor life, neither angels nor demons, neither our fears for today nor our worries about tomorrow—not even the powers of Hell can separate us from God's love. No power in the sky above or in the Earth below, indeed, nothing in all creation will ever be able to separate us from the love of God that is revealed in Christ Jesus, our Lord (Romans 8:31-39).

Autograph Page

Ms. Roberta Bell

Transformation: From the Inside Out

About the Author

Ms. Brittany Sullivan

Brittany Sullivan is from Indianapolis, IN. She is the mother of an eight-year-old name Trinity (TRIN-SETTA). Brittany graduated in 2006 from Arsenal Technical High School.

She has always wanted to write and get her word out to the world, she just never felt like she would find the right words. Since middle school, Brittany has written many stories, but would never finish them. Brittany always wonder, what people would think and how they would feel if they were to read her stories. Every time she was given an English assignment to write short stories, she would always ace them. Brittany always worked hard for everything that she wanted in her life, and she is always striving for greatness. The day she had her daughter, she knew that she needed to really wake up and make things happen for not only her future, but also her daughter's future.

Brittany loves traveling the world to see different things. Helping others as best as she can, which has always been a passion of hers. Brittany takes pride in making sure others around her are okay. She hopes and prays that her words touch the lives of many people and help them overcome whatever their struggle may be.

Transformation: From the Inside Out

Transformation: From the Inside Out

Acknowledgements

 First and foremost, I give thanks to God, who is the head of my life and who had my back through it all. Thank You for every single thing you took me through and all the ways that you brought me through them. Many nights I talked with You, and You showed me things that I didn't want to accept, but You helped me, stayed by my side, and never left me. I love You so much.

 I dedicate this book to my wonderful daughter, Trinity Monae. Baby, I pray that I'm raising you into the strong woman I know you can be. I pray that you never, ever get stuck inside of any situation that you can't get out of. I pray that you never let anything keep you bonded at your feet that makes you feel like you can't move. I will say this: I love you more than life itself, and the day I met you was the greatest day of my life. I never knew what true love was until the day that the doctor placed you in my arms and I heard your tiny cries. I knew that you were all that I truly needed. I still remember dressing you like my little baby doll and showing you off to the world. My lil Trin-Setta, you give me every reason to never give up. I will always put you before anyone else in this world. I pray for you all the time, and I hope you will always love me. I still remember the first time I cried in front of you, and you crawled into my arms and begin to wipe my tears away. From that day forward, I promised to never cry in front of you again, but instead simply make sure you see my hard work. Trin, everything I do now, I do it for you, honey. Through the ups and the downs, the ins and the outs: I promise to always guide you and to keep you from frowning. I love you, my angel. Thanks for coming into my life and giving me the one thing I was missing. I pray I never, ever lose you. We laugh together, cry together, eat together, sleep together, stress together, and are blessed together; but when I make it big, you will be set forever.

 To my nieces and cousin: I pray that y'all always come to me if you ever feel like you can't go to anyone else. I love y'all. To my sister, Tae and my brothers, Dre and Tonio: thanks for never turning y'all back on me even when I did things wrong. Thanks for protecting me and accepting me just as I am. Thanks for telling me that I shouldn't ever change for any one. I love y'all with all my heart.

To my two dear and strong black Queens: my mom, Gloria and my granny, Ghit (she's going to kill me for that!) I love you two with every last breath in me. Thanks for showing me how to survive on this Earth and for teaching me how to be a strong, black, independent woman. I thank you ladies for the many nights y'all prayed with me and helped me wipe away my tears. I will always have y'all embedded into my heart.

To my father: thanks for giving me a reason to write and help others. Thanks for doing your best now at trying to build a relationship with me and Trin. I will always love you no matter what you may think.

To my aunts Donna, Shell, and Mary (Rih): thanks for all the laughs, for always being there for me when I needed y'all most, and for always having my back no matter what. Family is truly forever, and I pray that y'all never leave me. Thanks for helping me grow into someone who never gives up, but simply pushes through.

To my beloved boo, my King, Anton: Thanks for supporting me through the many nights I complained and didn't take myself seriously. Thanks for all the encouraging words that you have ever given me. Thanks for always having my back, even through the ups and the downs that we been though. I love you, and I always thank God for our journey. You taught me to slow down and love wholeheartedly, even when I didn't want to.

I dedicate this book to all the women who are stuck inside of anything that isn't helping them grow. I pray that this really helps you.

Last but not least, I dedicate this book to ME. I pray I never ever get stuck inside of depression, hurt or sorrow ever again. During my writing, I gave up at least five times before I finally went through with finishing. It was like when I talked about it, it came out beautifully, but on paper, it wasn't coming out right. I began to pray and press. I claimed the things I wanted and God began to show

Transformation: From the Inside Out

me all the right things that had been in my face the whole time. I pray that I always remember You and put You before anyone. I thank you for never giving up. I love you more than life itself. Know this: WHEN YOU SIT DOWN YOUR WORDS WILL STAND UP!

Transformation: From the Inside Out

Transformation: From the Inside Out

Stuck

Inside of Who She Is, Who She Was, and Who She is Becoming!

Sit up straight, ladies!! Time to wake up, pay attention, and really focus! Have you ever found yourself in a situation that was hard to get out of, or in a place where you no longer wanted to be? Have your ever wanted to do something, but feared the thought of rejection or your past coming back to haunt you? We've all been there before, but didn't know what that feeling was or how to overcome it. That feeling that you feel is a *stuck* and *settling* feeling. What is *stuck* you ask? *Stuck* means unable to move from a particular position or unable to change a situation. Or, in my words, bonded inside broken dreams. Get up now and go to the mirror. No, really, get up off your butt and go to the mirror. Ask yourself, "Am I a *stuck* woman?" Now, really think about this situation because lot of women don't even realize that they're *stuck* and *settling* until it's already too late. No matter how great we think our lives are going, at times we feel like we want more, but we are too scared of rejection, failure, and sometimes even loneliness. Why do we fear things so much, ladies? Why are we letting the thought of fear keep us from our goals? The best thing in the world is getting to know yourself and loving yourself. It's time for a major change in order to regain our queen titles back. I'm here because I care, and at one time in my life I was a *stuck* woman, also. I was stuck inside hurt, depression, and heartache. One day, I realized it was time to let go of the things I can't control and to get away from my fears. So today, I'm here to help someone help themselves. I'm here to encourage you, while also encouraging myself, uplifting myself, and building myself.

Ladies, we must stop ourselves from falling into traps that are leaving us so *stuck* and really take pride in the women we are, who we are becoming, and who we are destined to be. Let's gain a better future for ourselves. Let's gain back our confidence and pride. Look in the mirror again, and ask yourself these three things: Are you happy? Can you do better? Are you where you want to be in life? Take the time to seriously think about these questions and to really take a look at the things going on around you. I can remember asking myself these same questions a few years back. Before I knew it, I was crying, because I wasn't happy, I wanted more, and I wasn't where I wanted to be in life. No matter how badly we don't want to face facts, a lot of us are *stuck* and *settling* inside situations that we don't even have to be in. Ladies, it's time for us to wake up and make a change. It's time to fill our life back up with blessings and happiness. There are many ways that we can remove ourselves out of hurt, pain, and even misery! The first step is admitting we are *stuck* and wanting to get out of the situation that has us *stuck*. We are letting these things control us and make us bitter. Let's leave a world of things that have us *stuck,* and let's go into a world that is leaving us *stuck*.

    The first thing that has us *stuck* is our past. So many of us have been through a lot of pain, and a lot of us are still stuck in that pain from the past. We're letting the pain control us and keep us in a positon that won't ever change until we make the change. Have you ever found yourself always thinking of the hurt from your past? Have you ever found yourself wishing things from your past can change? Have you ever regretted some decisions you once made? LET IT GO! We walk around with such heavy burdens on our hearts and even our bodies. Our past is starting to determine our future. It's past time to make a change and grow into the strong woman God put you on this Earth to be. Take back that control the devil is trying his hardest to keep from you. Why keep letting things we can't control take over the things that we can get in control? It's time to move forward from that past that has been haunting you and leaving you in a *stuck* situation. No more letting what the past did to us control us and have power over us.

    The past was always my biggest problem when I was going through my *stuck* and *settling* phase. I had to really grow and learn that I can't control my past, but I sure can change my present and future. I began to look at the people around me that reminded me of my past, and removed them from my life. I had to forgive some that hurt me and pray for a better heart and mind. I always battled with abandonment issues since I was a little girl who grew up with a pop-up dad most of my life. What's a pop-up dad you ask? Someone who may show up and may not. Growing up this way always left me *stuck*. For a very long time, I blamed my dad for all the situations and bad things that ever happened to me. I was pissed knowing that he wasn't there when I needed him most. For a long time, I prayed for a better father or even just a father figure that would help me. I blamed God for giving me this man that was not man enough to take care of his child as a father. Yes, he could've been a better father and man, but who knows maybe he was *stuck* also. Maybe he feared fatherhood, and didn't know how to raise a child. I later learned to stop blaming him for me being in my stuck situation. Not having him around was supposed to give me that much more reason to push harder and go after everything my heart needed and desired. The more I blamed him, the harder it was to get out of my situation. After years of not having him, I became this strong woman that believed I didn't need a man to make me into the woman I wanted to become. Besides, I had two great brothers who taught me about the things I needed to look out for. I was sitting back blaming everybody for the things I was going through when I should have been blaming myself. I no longer walk around with the weight of the world on my shoulders and I no longer carry burdens that are out of my control. Have you ever blamed someone for your life issues? Time to get out of that stage and remember who you are. I was sinking in the quicksand of life, drowning myself with the pain and hurt from my pop-up dad. I stopped trying to get to know him and worrying about him as much as I did, but I wanted him around because he was supposed to be my first true love. I'm now able to call him and tell him I love him, and he always calls me just to tell me he loves me and to ask about my daughter. Don't get me wrong, we still have a lot of growing to do, but I'm glad I removed the hate

Transformation: From the Inside Out

from my heart and replaced it with the love he's trying to give me now.

Go back to your mirror. Once again, get up off your butt and go look in the mirror. Say this with pride, "I GOT THIS!" How did that make you feel? Probably just a little bit better. Okay ladies, I want you to write down three things from your past that have you stuck. When you write them down, I want you to ask yourself, "Were any of these things anything you could control?" Most likely they were not things that you could really control. Now, I want you to concentrate on how you can reverse your past to make a better future for yourself. Think about how many blessings you may have missed out on by letting life hold you back from your plans for this long. Ladies, it's really time to regroup, rethink, and reevaluate the things that are inside of your life leaving you stuck and bonded. These are the three R's of life. When we begin to regroup, we are gathering ourselves back on the right track and leading ourselves to greater things in life. When we regroup, we are reassembling ourselves and rearranging our lives and the things that are causing our *stuck* situations. Begin regrouping when you feel like things around you aren't in place. Have you ever been so off-balanced with life that you have to come back to center within yourself? When you begin to regroup you are getting your life back to where you want it to be. When we begin to rethink, we are taking the time to think through our mess and how we can stay away from going back. We are thinking of ways that we can help ourselves overcome our past and change it to a better future. We are thinking carefully about things and people around us that do not have our best interest at heart. Rethinking gives you room to expand the boundaries that you have set for yourself. Remember, there is no limits or boundaries to life. Go for whatever it is that you have your mind set on, and watch the blessings in your life start expanding. Blessing and favor. When we reevaluate, reevaluating everything around us from friendships that are sour to relationships that are damaging to us, we are taking a step back from things that are causing us pain, hurt, and discomfort. Also, we are leaving behind things like grief, heartache,

Transformation: From the Inside Out

and sorrow. When you reevaluate your life, you are leaving who isn't doing you any good anymore. If they aren't helping you grow, then leave them behind and focus on what's better for you. It's time to be about our business, ladies. When we reevaluate things we are determined to set value on the things we want to come forth and grow. Plant those seeds within you and watch them grow and blossom with lots of prayer and guidance. Now, ask yourself, do you need to regroup, rethink, and reevaluate anything in your life or anything around you? Most of us women will have to do all three. Go to the mirror again. Okay, you're gonna make me buy you a mirror since you don't want to get up off your butt. I want you to go to the mirror and say, "I GOT THIS AND I CAN DO IT." How did that make you feel? Just knowing that you can handle anything that comes your way. It feels great knowing you can do whatever you put your mind to. Every day and night, I want you to tell yourself that and watch how things around you begin to change. Being bonded to your past begins to make you settle, you may even start settling for things that bring you down deeper into depression. Now is the time to snatch our lives, our future, and our self-respect back. Stop losing yourself in the past you, and focus more on who you are now and where you are trying to go. WAKE UP!!!

    Ladies, let's talk about another thing that has us so *stuck*: relationships and friendships. In life, we must learn to remove ourselves from things that are no any longer healthy for us. These two things are the main things that are making us feel down and in pain. Open up your mind, I want you to really think about these two things. Have you settled inside of a relationship thinking you can change the person or that the person will change? If you say no, then good, but most of us have settled inside a relationship that has hurt us, stressed us out, and left us depressed. I, myself, have been in damaging relationships and friendships more then I should've been. I've stayed at times thinking, hoping and wishing the person would change and love me just as much as I loved them. They never did. If someone isn't giving you 100% like you are giving them, move on! That person doesn't have your best interest at heart and doesn't care about you as much as you care about them. I want you to ask yourself three things: Is this relationship healthy? Does this person make me better? Since I've been around this person have I grown? Now, don't just think about the partying and the lovemaking. Really ask yourself these questions wholeheartedly, and be honest with yourself. If you haven't seen improvement in your life or growth while in a relationship or friendship, guess what? It's time to truly let it go so you can have the time and space for the things that do make you grow. Now, it doesn't have to just be your friends or your mate. It could be your family, your job, and anything else you haven't seen growth in. I once learned from a close friend of mine, "Not everyone around you wants to change and once you start to change and grow you will notice who is ready to grow and who never will."

    Ladies, if anybody you hang with is still doing the same thing that you once did when you were younger and in high school, guess what? Yes, you guessed it, it's time to let them go and find better friends that will help you grow. Okay, go to the mirror again. Well, since you still being lazy go to your camera and ask yourself: "Am I doing the same thing I was doing when I was in high school?" "Have I grown since high school?" If you are over the age of twenty-five and you're still doing things you once did at eighteen or twenty-one, its time to wake up, wise up, and grow up. Be about your business, ladies, and get on your job. If the relationship is causing you more grief, depression, and misery use the 3 R's of life and move on. Relationships aren't always supposed to be sunshine and rainbows, but if you are seeing more thunderstorms and hail inside of your relationship it's time to put your lifejacket on and jump off the ship. I've had a few women around me that settled because they didn't feel worthy of anything better and feared that they wouldn't find better. Wrong! You are very much worthy of anything that God has for you. Never, ever be with a person that has you wondering if you're good enough for him or her. There are a lot of men out here in the world that are *stuck* as well, and they'll try to do anything to bring you down. Never let someone drag you deep into something that has you looking stupid and walking around being his friends' or family's joke. A lot of us notice the signs, we just do our best to ignore them just to say we have someone there at night or someone who we think is our own. Take the time out to become the person you want to be before you allow another man or woman to destroy the temple you're trying to build. Ask yourself, have you stayed in a relationship because you don't feel worthy of better or greater? Have you stayed out of fear that nobody else will want you? Have you stayed because you feel like you can't be great without the person? If for any reason all the questions fit you, then it's really time to step back and create a better surrounding for yourself. I've stayed in relationships for all the wrong reasons before and I've *settled* because I became content to the pain that I was going through. I began to numb my body of hurt and sweep most things under the rug, hoping that the person I was with would change for the better. I waited for him to hurt me more than enough times before I finally gave up on what we once had. Now, don't get me wrong, walking away isn't always as easy as we want it to be. As much as we hate to admit it, we all have stayed somewhere we shouldn't have been or did something we shouldn't have. We have all given second chances to friendships and relationships. I was once talking to my older sister and I told her, "People are not perfect, it's okay to give more than one chance." She told me, "I gave chances for a very long time. I know what I want now, and I can't keep giving people my power and energy. So, no I cannot give out any more chances." I said, "But people make mistakes and it's ok to accept things." She said, "No, it's not okay to accept things, because then you will continue to let those things slide." She made a great point. She was basically telling me that by accepting things all the time I would end up settling for whatever and that would leave me *stuck*. It hurts to know that sometimes we've stayed stuck so long inside a broken friendship or broken relationship that we are numbing and dumbing ourselves down just to be with them. If that person doesn't check on you just as much as you do them, you should slowly begin to remove yourself. If that person isn't there for you as much as you are for them, slowly remove yourself. If that person is always seeing the worst in you and never the good, slowly remove yourself from them and start seeing the best in yourself. No more dumbing ourselves down for the likes of being in a relationship or friendship.

Trust me when I say if it doesn't make you better, doesn't help you grow, or doesn't take you places higher than where you are now, leave! Even though it might not seem like love is real nowadays and like relationships don't last now that sex is so easy, there is someone out here that is ready and waiting to receive you as their queen. They are ready to love you and appreciate you as the woman God made you to be. They could be out there *stuck* just like you are. They might be scared to fall in love with fear of being hurt. Another issue we have that keeps us stuck is how we handle the things we can't change. We take so much time trying to change things that are impossible to change that we are no longer able to focus on the greater part of us. We try our best to change people around us as well as the past things that have happened to us, but the best thing we can change is ourselves and the person we are. We can't keep going back and forth with things that leave us *stuck* and defeated. I've been in situations where I went back and forth fighting myself over why my life was the way it was. I was slowly failing Brittany by focusing too much on trying to make others better. I didn't save room for myself and the growth that I needed to succeed in life. I was not growing nor was I learning anything. Remember ladies, not everything can be fixed and not everything is meant to be repaired. Stop trying to change the unchangeable.

Change within yourself first; that is the first step to recovery and regrowth. When you start to see a change within yourself, then the things around you begin to change, which leaves less room for stress or depression. Evaluate the things around you that left you down, and change it to make things in your life much better. Leave no room for a stressful life or environment. Let go of whatever isn't bringing growth, and focus on a better you. Its okay to change from the inside first, because once you have an interior growth then your exterior will automatically want the change as well. Change into the warm, cuddly butterfly you want to be.

FEARS

Let's talk about a few fears that have us *stuck* and scared to grow in life. We have so many fears in life: fear of rejection, fear of change, fear of not being good enough, fear of things not working out. I could go on and on about our many fears. We often fear what others may think, or if they will be mad at us. If we continue to live our life this way, we will never make it out of our situation. This isn't a book about a certain race, but instead a book for all races. We all have been at a point where we were unhappy before. We, as women, face many challenges. A lot of us can handle the challenges, but at the same time a lot of us can't because we don't know how to deal with them. We give up, place them in the back of our minds, and sweep them under the rug until they resurface again. A lot of us hide our burdens from the world by showing them our clown faces. We're busy putting on a front when we really just need to let go of the pain and move on with our lives. No, I'm not saying it's easy to get over pain, because trust me, it's not. Getting over things takes time. Some things take months, even years and it's not as easy to walk away from the things that you are so used to. When your heart is tired, you will know, because your body will become numb and nothing the person does or says will even bother you anymore.

Rejection is one of the fears in life we need to focus less on. We must stop thinking that every 'no' is the end and feeling that nothing better is going to come along for us. For every single 'no', there will come a 'yes'. Prayer and belief within yourself can get you a long way. Just stop and think about how many times Oprah was told 'no' only to finally get that one break that led her to a life of greatness. I know she must have wanted to give up and just stop, but her drive kept her going to see the bigger picture in life. Letting rejection stop you from doing things you always wanted to do will leave you stuck and unsatisfied. Personally, whenever someone would tell me no about something, I went that much harder for what I wanted. I always used their 'no' or 'maybe' as a reason to attack the battle given to me that much stronger. At this stage is when you go straight to your mirror and say, "I got this and I will do it." No more giving up or giving in, just keep going and striving to see that bigger picture. Rejection should be removed from your thought process and your life.

Change is the second fear that is leaving us in a life full of pain and making us stay *stuck* in our situation. We fear that if we grow, then the people around us will look at us differently or start judging us. Who cares what others may think about us; we have to be about our business for only ourselves and no one else. It's truly okay to change and grow. It's ok to lose friends that never want to see the greatness that you are starting to see in yourself. Stop settling for these broken friendships and these damaging relationships that are causing you to forget the woman you are. Ladies, we must create space for growth. Rid yourself of your old ways of not wanting to change because of the fear that you will lose friends, family, or even yourself. This is all part of the growth process that we need in order to change ourselves and rid ourselves from the toxic waste life can bring upon us. Remember, sometimes you have to lose friends in order to grow. Not everybody is meant to grow and expand with you. Change must be something you truly want to do. Don't think about others and how they are going through life. Change isn't a bad thing, because it help us look back on the things we have been doing and notice all the time we have been wasting by staying down in our sorrow. Change helps us learn who we are and helps us to become a better mother, sister, friend, and person.

Loneliness is the deepest fear we, as women, deal with. We are terrified by the thought of being alone and the thought of no one being around to love us. News flash: love yourself, encourage yourself, believe in yourself, take time to know yourself, and be with yourself. Until you learn to love the person you are, no one else will take the time to get to know you and love you either. A lot of women are settling in damaging relationships because they can't take the thought of being alone. I had to learn that it is truly okay to be alone and to stop looking for others to fill the void that was in my life. Once I learned to fill the void with my own love and happiness, I began to grow into the woman I was truly destined to be. I had to stop making time for people that never really took the time out for me. I had to stop being there for people who could never be there for me. I had to stop dropping everything for people who wouldn't drop anything for me. Guess what began to happen? I began to lose people. You know, most people are around as long as you are doing something for them, but the minute you stop catering to them and being there for them is when they have so much to say about you. I began to take myself on dates, hang out with myself, and love on myself. Telling you that you will never find another person or you will never be much without them. Making you feel unworthy and not good enough. The threats of them moving on without you leave you scared of being alone, but once again, it is truly okay to be alone. I repeat, IT'S TRULY OKAY TO BE ALONE! No matter how much it hurts, no matter how hard it is to accept the loneliness, deal with it and grow. Don't wait until after the man or woman has hurt you over and over again to realize that you were better off without them years ago. One of the worst people you can ever sleep on in this world is yourself. Once you begin to sleep on yourself, then everyone else around you will begin to do the same thing. Love yourself, value yourself, and respect yourself enough to walk away and never look back. Accept the loneliness around you or start meeting new people.

  Learn to take the time out for yourself. Here's an exercise I want you to do with yourself once a month: I don't care what you do, I want you to get up, fix yourself up, and take yourself on a date. Have a little alone time to yourself. You can take yourself anywhere, but make sure that you are going somewhere out of the house—even if it's just a walk in the park. Even if you're married, in a relationship or whatever it's called nowadays—treat yourself. When you begin to do these things, you will learn how much it means to be alone and without others. The greatest feeling in the world is learning who you are and what you are put on this Earth to be. Go on out and love on yourself, ladies! The day that you get over the fears of life that are leaving you stuck and inside a settling, damaging relationship will be the day you see many things around you begin to change for the better. Greater is coming to us, ladies. Trust me, we just have to really put our mind to it and accept that greater is coming for us.

MISTAKES

Let's speak on a few mistakes that leave us stuck and make us settle. First off, there are many mistakes that keep us stuck and bonded to the things that are out of our control. The first mistake we have made is not taking our instincts seriously. If you ever feel like you can do something and that you got it, then go for it! There is no need to doubt yourself. Never allow what others say you can't do to stop you from achieving your goals that you set in life. Sometimes we don't believe in our first instincts and things never go right. I was always a person who doubted my hard work. I would get nervous and think that I would fail, and I even started to believe that I was a failure. I was speaking things into my life that weren't even there in first place. I had to talk to someone very powerful for them to tell me that the tongue speaks life and death, and I cannot worship a lie that I was trying to tell myself. The less I believed in myself, the more others began to see that I didn't.

The second mistake we have is labeling our efforts. The more you give something a try, the better life will be. If you always give up on things, then you will see the same results over and over again. A lot of times we think we aren't good enough to get or receive better in life, and we begin to tell ourselves that we are stupid or the things that we are trying to build are stupid. We sit around negative people that aren't helping us, but that are simply keeping us down. Stop being scared to go after what is out there for you; and most definitely stop caring about what others would think and use your heart and mind to go after every single thing in life. No more second guessing yourself, as of today. I always used to ask people, "Why do you keep going back to the same situation that had you stuck, sad, depressed, and in a lot of pain? Why even stay in that situation?" They would tell me, "It's a love thing, you will never understand." I never fully understood that love was that deep to make you stay in pain and heartache. I guess at the time I was asking these people I was too young to understand and get what they were going through. I was always judging them and telling them how I think it's crazy to stay somewhere as damaging as that. Funny and crazy thing is that years later, I had to deal with the same thing that they called love and the issues that they dealt with. I began settling inside broken relationships, not because I didn't love me, but because I didn't love me enough. I stayed for the child, I stayed because of what others may think, and I stayed because at the time, I didn't want to be alone. I stayed because, at times, that void filled the pain my father should have filled. I began to settle inside of feeling like I couldn't find better. I began to settle inside of pain, hurt, and misery. But worst of all, I stayed because I didn't want him to find better than me. I didn't realize that he would be missing out on me—not the other way around. I was the best, even if he never thought I was good enough. I was the best.

    It's funny how I could always give people some of the best advice and some of the greatest quotes, but yet I was going home sad and depressed in my own relationship. Crazy how you can help others without even realizing that you were helping yourself. Love will make you do some crazy things if you aren't careful. It will have you out here blind to everything that is damaging to you and your life. Trust me, ladies, I had one on one talks with God asking him to remove people from me that aren't any good for me. I would also ask him to show me if the person is right for me, and each time he showed me. Now, ladies, know this: When you ask God to show you something, He will show you. However, it's up to you to listen and take heed to what He is showing you and the people He is removing. It's up to you to want to walk away. The only thing God can do is show you what you asked of Him and help you have the strength to remove them. Once you begin to remove those damaging, draining people from your life, leave them out of your life. No matter what you do, don't begin to settle into damaging relationships, friendships, or even family situations again. Pay attention to the people around you that mean you no good. Remember, being content in a situation can have you stuck as well.

BREAK FREE

Let's get a few things straight. When we are bonded by things that leave us *stuck,* we get weighed down by these things as well. It always seems like when you are going through things everyone around you is moving at a fast pace, living their life, while you are being held back by cement bricks around your ankles. It keeps us down, and we begin to get angry. We get angry not only with ourselves, or the people around us, but also with God. We begin to take our anger out on Him, believing there must be someone stronger out there that can help us. Trust me, I have questioned God a lot of times in my life. I began losing my faith and trust in Him. I began believing I could handle all things without him, and sadly enough, I was mistaken. Often times, I looked for people to help me, support me, and build me up. I was thinking if the man I praise every week couldn't help, then there had to be another power. Wrong! I thought, *why get on bended knees if my situation wasn't changing? Why keep giving my tithes and offering to a church if the man who I was praying with every night wasn't helping me*? I was mad at God and blaming Him, when in all honesty, he showed me what I needed to be shown. I was ignoring what he was showing me, because I didn't want to lose what he was showing me. Stop looking for people to be there for you and start being there for yourself. Believe me, nothing without Christ can grow. We need that extra amount of praise and prayer. Why give God five percent and give people who hardly even care ninety-five percent? It just doesn't work that way.

Stop looking for handouts and the likes of others to show you the way. Half the time those same people could care less whether you are growing or not. Have you ever wondered why people who barely know you support you more than people who have known you for years? The reason people who don't know you support you is because they don't know your story or your past, they only see the greatness you show them. People who know you often times wonder how it's possible for you to grow when they are stuck in the same spot. They want you to remain down on your luck, and half of them don't want you to pass them by and leave them. They fear you will forget about them, so they often times tell you that you can't or shouldn't do something. Leave these type of people to themselves, they truly mean you no good.

Why must we be so jealous of each other? And don't say you've never been jealous, because we have all been jealous at one time in our lives. Most won't even admit it. Why be jealous of each other's growth, especially our fellow sisters? What happen to encouraging one another, building each other up, and helping each other grow? We concentrate so much on kicking each other while we are down instead of helping each other get to where we are going in life. Time to unite, uplift, and build with our sisters. Time to show them that at least someone has their back in life. Ladies, okay, I want you to do an exercise for me this month. The next few ladies you meet, I want you to go to them, smile, and tell them, "You got it and you can do it." They may look at you weird or even frown at you, but simply explain to them what you are talking about. Let them know that it's okay to not be in control of things, but instead to handle all things through Christ who strengthens them. Even if they don't understand right then and there, later they will know that they can do it and that they got it. Let them know that God has a blessing with their name on it if they are ready to receive it. For your information, ladies, you can do it. Just take your time, and remember slow process is better than no process. It's better to go out on the battling field with your full armor on than to be wasting away and letting life pass you by.

That's the first step to growth into your new life. It will not only make you feel better, but others around you will feel better as well. You will begin to gain a bond within yourself and trust in yourself that even you didn't know you could build. Encouragement builds us up, ladies. Just to know that someone else can see that you can do it makes you feel that much better in life. Sometimes all we need to hear is a single word, and our day will be that much better. Encouragement from others and even yourself makes you feel like you can take over the world. You never truly know what someone is going through, and simply telling them that they can do something will probably change their whole week. Your encouragement may even open their eyes and have them focusing on what it is that they themselves need to change, as well.

Ever listen to that song "Encourage Yourself"? Well, in life, you must encourage yourself enough to be able to encourage, uplift, and build the courage of other women around you. Okay, let's have some fun now. What is something about yourself that needs encouragement? Go to the mirror again and tell yourself, "I love you no matter what." Build up your self-esteem so no man or woman can tear it down. Smile at your mirror, strike a pretty pose, capture the moment, and go get it printed out and framed. Hang it somewhere on your mirror, and remember that moment and how it made you feel forever. Always go back to that place of loving yourself.

LIES WE TELL OURSELVES

In life, we let what society tells us is wrong attack our minds and our bodies. We are told that we aren't tall enough, we aren't skinny enough, we aren't light enough, our hair isn't long enough, our butts aren't big enough, and our lips aren't thick enough. And when the world is shaming what you call beauty and making you feel like you're not good enough, you start believing it. This is where the lies begin to set in. The lies we tell ourselves will keep us stuck inside of our situation and not able to grow. At times, we don't feel like we are good enough and that we won't amount to anything. We are truly wrong. We can amount to so much if we stop listening to what society is telling us to do, and stop comparing ourselves to what we see on social media and the Internet. Stop focusing on things you hate about yourself, and focus more on the things you love the most. Name three parts of you that you love the most. Why do you love these parts of you? What are ways that you can always focus on these three main parts? There's no need to be walking around not loving the person that God brought into this world. Always remember, someone else's trash is someone's greatest prized treasure.

    Trust me, some of the people you see on the Internet and idolize so much live the most miserable lives. They just know how to not look like what they've been through; they know how to carry themselves. We lie to ourselves saying we live a good enough life, so we settle inside of situations and stop craving the better that we truly need and want. We believe that since others around us haven't gotten out of the situation that they're in, we can't either. But who knows what others are doing? Maybe they are lying to themselves, as well believing that better won't come, or that they are doing good enough when they're really not. Others may be being lazy and not really wanting to see their greatness because of the rejection that they have faced time and time again. We lie by not telling our stories or the things we are going through. Sad thing is, there are people out there going through the same thing or even similar things that you are going through, but they're also scared to share their story. Lying to yourself will not change your present situation, it will only hinder you from growing into a better you. When you settle inside of a lie, the pain only gets worse as time goes on. Nothing seems to go the way we will want it to go, and then that's where heartache sets in. What are some things that you lie to yourself about? What are ways that you can get away from the lies you tell yourself? How often do you lie to yourself? It's time to stop lying to yourself and be about your business, ladies. Time you get *unstuck* and *away from settling*.

CHANGE FROM THE INSIDE OUT

We have to learn to start taking ourselves seriously or no one else in this world will ever give you a shot. Remember, first impressions are everything to people, and sometimes you only get that one shot. This month, ladies, I want you to take the time out and find your personal style, the way you want to look, and the way you'd like to dress. You have to be about yourself and fix what needs to be fixed. I have a few tips and things that you must do in order to change into the person that you are trying to become. We must make sure our interior matches our exterior. Cleanse yourself inside out and work on a greater you. Keep in mind that change may also cause you to lose friends or it could help others around you grow with you. It's okay to leave them if they're not willing to go to the next level with you. If they don't want a better future, let them know that you want greater and you will have to leave them in order to get to the level of life you want to go.

The first step to making a change is appearance. Okay, ladies, it's time to take off them scarves, change out of those pajamas, comb out your hair, and even let go of hats as your daily routine. No more walking around like you just jumped fresh out the bed. Now don't get me wrong, I be wanting to be in comfy girl mode all the time; but if I want people around me to take me seriously as the professional, strong woman that I am, then I have to give up a few things. The first way to change is within ourselves. Showing the world who we are becoming is hard sometimes. You will have people around you that will always bring up the old you. They will always try to challenge the new change you are trying to show the world. Remember one thing only: this new journey isn't about them, it's all about me now. Yeah, I know, at times it is hard to go to the beauty shop and clothing store to get things, especially if you got kids. I know we don't always have the money for the things that we truly want and need. Let me help you work on those things and show you the things that helped me when I was breaking through from my *stuck* situation.

YouTube has so many channels you can look up and find yourself some kind of style that you can do yourself. It even has people shopping in different thrift shops and buying nice things, putting them together as well. Make sure you are being about your business. A little extra change in your check can allow you to go buy a shirt, a pair of pants, or a nice pair of shoes. You don't have to walk around with the top brands on just get up. Get dressed and take back your self-esteem. Build up your courage and your personality that you once had. Taking yourself seriously and being about your business will let others see the wonderful person you've been hiding for so long. Grab that mirror and smile your prettiest smile. Take on the world with a nice blouse, new hairdo, or even just a big smile. This is an exercise I want you to do right when you get done reading this: I want you look through your clothes, grab three different outfits, piece them together based on what you really like, iron it, fix your hair, and if you like makeup, throw some on. Fix yourself, and take a picture with your brightest smile. Hold your head up high and say, "Girl, you look good." Confidence within yourself is the sexiest thing a woman can ever carry. Let's get it, ladies. Just giving a little can take you a very long way in life, but you must give that great first impression.

The next step to a wonderful change is changing the way you carry yourself. Remember, people are always listening. Be aware of the way you talk around people. Young people, find a better vocabulary, because older people are listening to you. They're putting all young people inside a group of people that don't listen, don't care, and that will die from lack of knowledge. Change the way you are talking to your kids. Stop hollering so much for all the things that you are supposed to do. Sometimes it's the way you carry yourself that pushes people away, you have to have respect

Transformation: From the Inside Out

for the people around you. Nobody takes the younger generation seriously anymore because we don't have respect for ourselves or for older people. We're cursing and being disrespectful around our older generation. It's a must that if you have younger children looking up to you that you teach them respect, and how to talk to their elders. Change the way you walk. Walk with your head held high, shoulders back, and a smile. Trust that people are going to talk about you anyways, so give them a reason to talk about you in a good way. Smile and speak, show them that God fearing queen you are.

    The next best thing you can do is to change your attitude. If you are always walking around or talking with some attitude, no one will ever know how to handle you. They will always think negative things of you and not be able to see who you truly are. Your attitude from the pain or something that you are going through will always come off wrong to someone who barely knows you. This is where they start labeling before they even get the chance to see who you are. I was always looked at as this mean person. I hardly smiled, and I always kept this certain mug on my face, even when I was happy. People would always label me according to this and when they finally talked to me or seen my silly side, this is when they saw the real me. I push a lot of people away with my attitude, and I lost a lot of people, some who loved me so much that they finally had to show me that my attitude was ugly. It hurts badly when you lose someone who you're so used to being able to call on or hang out with a lot, but due to the attitude that you give them, they finally have to walk away themselves. I didn't know how to explain to them that I wasn't giving them attitude. It was my attitude that pushed them away, and I had no one to blame but myself. No one is in control of your attitude but *you*. I will say this one more time, no one is in control of your attitude but *you*. People didn't know the true love I had for them, because my attitude was the only thing they were shown. It took me being alone to know that it was time to truly work on me from the inside out. I no longer do those things anymore, life is too short for it and someone close to me is dying every day. Have you ever pushed someone away with your attitude? Your independence? When you begin to change these things, your growth will shine through. Before you know it, your confidence will slowly begin to come back.

THE OVERCOMING

Ladies, as you attack life's journeys, I want you to start setting goals for yourself and within yourself. Start off with small goals, first. Make a list of some things you want to accomplish this year. Post sticky notes around your house with words of encouragement, small prayers, and even some of your favorite quotes. Begin to face your mirror every day, smile into it, show yourself the person who you are, then go out into the world and show it who you are as well. Take back what the devil tried so hard to steal from you, and claim every blessing that comes your way. Do everything you truly want to and never stop, no matter what. Make a vision board of the things you want to see in your life and hang it up in your room somewhere, and look at it every day. Find ways that you can accomplish everything on your list. Just never, ever give up.

Being that I was always looked on as this tough person, everybody always came to me and told me how strong I was, how powerful I was, and that I was very mature for my age. No one ever knew that even with me being so strong, I still had my weak moments. I could only be strong for so long, and no one ever knew that I needed someone to lean on. I didn't know how to share my story because I became afraid of what they may think. Will they think I'm weak? Will they think I couldn't handle it and try to look down on me? Will they take my conversation and give it to someone else? So I never shared with anyone anything about me. I would just listen to them and give as much positive feedback as I could. I would never let them know that I needed them just as much as they needed me. This left me stuck inside of my pain, my fears,

Transformation: From the Inside Out

and my heartache. I had fear of people judging me, downing me, and even talking about me behind my back. I didn't want to share with people the things about me. Yes, Brittany is strong, and yes, she can handle almost anything thrown her way. Did she need them like they needed her? Yes! I often times pushed people away that wanted to be there for me. They looked up to me and loved me, but I didn't truly know if what they gave me was real. I lost a lot of people that way.

Once I began to open up more, change the things around me, focus on my future, and on the new things that I wanted to see in my life, that's when I became free. I began to grow even stronger into the woman God put me on this Earth to be. I was grooming myself for a greater outcome and an even greater future. I was building myself up to be the leader that my daughter, nieces, and younger cousin need me to be. As I began to get myself together, I began to pray more, and I began to surround myself with more powerful people with the same drive and goals as me. I took pride in Brittany Sullivan and no longer let the stress of my past or damaged relationships and hurt get me down. Ladies, as I come to a close, if I taught you anything, I hope I taught you that you no longer have to deal with the issues of life alone and the things that life have brought into your life that are keeping you in a *stuck* situation. I hope I taught you that you can do all things through Christ that strengthens you, and that wonderful things will come into full force with Him by your side. I hope I taught you that even when we feel like we are alone and things aren't going our way, it is okay to lean on not only yourself, but also God. I know I wouldn't be as great of a woman without the thought of getting down on my knees and claiming everything that God had out there for me. I am a proud woman that has always chased after my goals, but now I know that things take time, and I can no longer rush the things I want. Instead, I simply take the time and let them come to me. Ladies, you can do anything in this world. There's one thing I ask that you don't do, and that's give up. Fellas, don't think you're off so quick, because you could be walking around *stuck,* but that would have to be a to-be-continued. Right, ladies?

Autograph Page

Ms. Brittany Sullivan

About the Author

Ms. Peggy Finkton

Peggy Finkton is a customer insurance representative and the founder of the "I Am My Sister's Keeper Book Club". She is a mother of two, has five grandchildren and one great-grandchild.

She is active in her church, The New Beginning Fellowship Church in Indianapolis, Indiana. She is a member of the Psalms of Judah Choir, a leader of small groups, and teaches new members and vacation bible school classes. Peggy loves studying and teaching the word of God.

In her spare time, she enjoys reading, sports and spending time with her family.

Transformation: From the Inside Out

Acknowledgements

First and foremost, I give all honor, glory and praise to my Heavenly Father. For without Him, I am nothing and can do nothing.

Then, I thank my niece, Minister Notoshia Howard, for asking me to be a part of this project. Even though I said I couldn't do it, she said, "Yes you can!" Thank you for the encouragement to step out on faith, and allowing God to stretch me in another direction.

Transformation: From the Inside Out

Transformation: From the Inside Out

THE JOURNEY

You are probably wondering why I called this "The Journey". I call this "The Journey" because that's exactly what it is: a journey back to you!

In Mark 10:8 concerning marriage, it says, "And the two shall become one flesh." Meaning there is no longer two individuals but a new unity is formed. The two of you have become one. His likes and dislikes become yours and vice versa. You share everything: your friends, your home, your finances, and everything else.

Life is rolling along and then come the situations that lead up to the divorce. Nobody gets married, spending lots of money in preparation for that day, just to become divorced. However, sometimes life just happens. Divorce can be one of the most devastating and life-changing events you will ever go through. After a divorce, you feel lost.

There are so many emotions you are dealing with: the shame, the hurt and the embarrassment. You are mad, angry, scared, alone and worried. You question your worth and value.

Sometimes the decision to divorce is yours, and sometimes it's not. People divorce for many reasons. Sometimes people just begin to head into different directions, growing apart.

Some people become bitter!

Some people become better!

There are so many things to consider and decisions that need to be made.

When making my decision to separate from my husband, it was a very rough time. Should I stay or should I go? How will this affect my daughter? How will I be able to make it? What will people say? How will he react? How will it affect our families, as they were very close?

I was going through a spiritual battle. The hardest part of making my decision was knowing I was not following the word of

Transformation: From the Inside Out

God. God adores marriage and He ordained it. During this time, I was crying and praying. I was reading my word and searching for the loophole in God's word to justify what I was contemplating doing. (I'm just being real, this is what we do when we want to justify our actions.) I continued to pray about my situation, and waited on God to change things and give me an answer.

During this time, I hadn't shared with anyone what I was going through or what I was thinking about doing. My battle was internal, though I was crying out on the outside. I remember my mother talking to me, because she thought I had been called to preach, and that's what was wrong with me.

But during this time, there were two things that happened that truly let me know that God will send people to minister to me or send a word through them.

The first thing that happened was this: I was in the basement at the church I attended at that time, and I was helping to tend to the minister who had just gotten through preaching. His wife and I were helping him, as he was still in the spirit. Out of nowhere, he turned to me and said "He's not going to change until he gets ready. I know because that was me until I truly turned my life over to God and He changed me." With his wife standing there, he began to share with me their story. I was just standing there listening, stunned, in disbelief thinking *how did he know about my situation*? It was like his wife could see what was going on with me, how her husband's words had struck a nerve with me. She spoke to me and said, "He has the gift that he can read people and see things."

This was the first time this had ever happened to me, so it really shook me up. To be honest, I didn't really believe in this, but then it happened again.

A friend of mine had invited me to her church for their women's day. There was a woman speaking there and when she got done she began to call people up and she began to read them. I thought *uh oh, time for me to go*. I didn't want to get up, because I didn't want to draw attention to myself. So I just sat there hoping she wouldn't call me up, but she did. She began to speak over me and then she said, "You've been crying and praying about what you've been dealing with, and God sees your tears. He said you're going to be alright." She told me how I was faithful in my church, but I wasn't happy there (which was also true), and then she said "and those life insurance policies you have, do not cancel them." I got scared and she said, "I'm not talking about somebody dying." I hit the floor.

Like I said before, I had not told anyone about what I was dealing with. To have two different people speak over my life and my situation was overwhelming. The pastor of that church directed me to read the book of Corinthian, regarding the gifts.

In the meantime, things had not changed in my marriage. After much prayer, I made the decision to separate from my husband. I found an apartment near my mother's house, and my daughter and I moved. When I moved, I only had my daughter's bedroom furniture, a dining room set, and a few other household items. I didn't even have a bed. I felt since I was the one leaving, I had no right to tear up that household to set up mine. Thank God for my family, who had a housewarming party for me and provided me with a lot of household items that I needed.

This was a very hard time. He didn't take it well, so that in itself was an issue. It's not easy when you are used to having someone in your life to spend time with and do things with, and then there is no one. You are used to having two incomes in the home, and now there is just one. Things you never had to worry about before like car repairs, moving heavy furniture, hanging a picture and just taking out the trash all become issues.

You worry about your friendships. The friends that you met through him, are they still your friends or not? The couples you associated with, what now?

My emotions were all over the place, and I was losing weight. I felt like I made the best decision for me, yet I was still an emotional wreck. I cried all the time. I remember my best friend, telling me it was okay to cry, and that I would cry more than that before it was over. I was mad and angry, because I felt if he loved me enough he would be willing to work on the issues we were having. Not all the issues were his.

At this time, mind you, we were just separated. During this time, God began to deal with me. He began to show me things about me. He was stretching me and showing me that if I belonged to Him, there was a standard I had to walk in. No matter what was going on, I couldn't act ugly.

Then there are the people in your life who say, "Girl, you should take the house." Or they say, "You should do this, and you should do that." I'm so glad I was listening to God and not people. God truly provided and kept me during this time.

One night, I was lying in bed and praying to God about how I was going to pay my bills. I was struggling and my mind was working overtime trying to figure out what I was going to do. I fell asleep and that night something woke me up, and I heard the words "those insurance policies".

Earlier I told you how the woman of God spoke over my life at that church service and she told me not to cancel those insurance policies.

Then I realized it was God waking me, giving me the answer to my prayer. The next morning, I called the insurance company and I was advised there was cash money that was available to me. Isn't God good?

God continued to work on me helping me get over being mad, hurt and angry about my marriage. He continued to speak to me about having the right attitude and mindset, and how I needed to respond to my husband when we had contact. How I had to reflect who I was in Him at all times.

After years of being separated, we got divorced. By then, we could come together and decide how we would handle things. We both had attorneys, but it was really just on paper.

It's funny, because even my attorney wanted me to go hard and take all that I could. She laid out all of my options. I even had to sign off on paper that she advised me of certain things, but I declined.

Transformation: From the Inside Out

One thing I could say is that just because we were not together, he never stopped taking care of his daughter. For that reason, I was not letting even my attorney cause me to act or do anything that was not pleasing to God.

Even though we are divorced, my ex-husband and I are the best of friends now. Shortly after the divorce, my ex-husband apologized for everything and then he said "The way I was acting, if I were you, I would hate me and wouldn't be speaking to me." And I had to let him know that it wasn't me, but the God within me. That He wouldn't let me act that way, but that I had to stand and be the church that is inside me.

Since the divorce, my ex-husband and I have been able to co-parent our daughter. Whatever we needed, he was there to provide. If I needed anything, I just needed to ask. He felt whenever I was in need it ultimately affected his daughter. Our daughter played basketball all her life, and we were able to travel together to wherever she played, even when she went off to college.

It's hard for people to believe that we are divorced but can still be around each other, go places and do things as friends. Most divorced people can't stand each other and almost hate each other. They spend their time trying to make life miserable for the other person at whatever cost. They are bitter and depressed. I'm so glad that I have God in my life, and that I can truly say He is the head of my life.

When you say God is the head of your life, get ready because He will take you on the journey of your life.

I thank God for the journey back to me. For being there to let me know, there is life after the divorce. For letting me know my value and worth to Him. That He loves me and will always be there for me.

Transformation: From the Inside Out

Autograph Page

Ms. Peggy Finkton

About the Author

Pastor Michele Miller

Michele Miller is a case coordinator for a non-profit organization where she mentors and advocates for the youth and provides life skills to young parents. She is the assistant pastor of Destiny Christian Tabernacle alongside her husband, who is the senior pastor of the ministry. Michele has a Bachelor of Science degree in Business Management and Ethics. She is a current student at Liberty University, pursuing her Masters of Arts degree in Human Services Counseling with a concentration in Crises Response and Trauma. Michele and her husband Bruce reside in Indianapolis, Indiana and together have five children; Dayon, Jason (Revae), Nicoya, Desiree (deceased), and Aundrea. She's the proud "mimi" of four granddaughters and a thankful co-owner of a German Shepard, Rubi.

Transformation: From the Inside Out

Acknowledgements

This book is being dedicated to my beautiful family; my husband Bruce and daughter Aundrea. My bonus children Dayon, Jason, and Nicoya; daughter-in-law, Revae, and my granddaughters, Nakayla, Ariana, Jaida and Savannah. You are all my greatest supporters and encouragers. My life would be so incomplete if you were not a part of it. I love you all so much! My extended family and "All the Way" team, Bishop Dewayne and Wanda Phelps, and my pastors, Bishop J. Laverne and Linda Tyson, for being with me during my grieving process. My healing process would have been twice as long without your support. My mentors, Apostle Mark and Prophetess Shalonda Kelley, and my coaches, Bishop Paul and Pastor Tara Thompson, thank you so much for your prayers and words of encouragement. You will never know how much of a "life" saver you all have been to me. My friends, Pastors Eddie and Notoshia Howard, for this opportunity and restoring my passion for writing again. The Destiny Christian Tabernacle Church family for your patience and understanding of my many "hats".

I write this book in loving memory of my daughter Desiree Nicole Miller.

Transformation: From the Inside Out

A Look Back to Move Forward

I remember the first time we heard the news of your arrival. I can recall the many emotions that were going through me. However, the greatest emotion I felt was that of fear. I feared the uncertainties of my carrying you. I feared that I was not going to be the mother that you need me to be. As I watched the news every morning as I was preparing for work, I could not help but notice all the negative current events taking place across the globe. As reporters discussed the national concerns of terrorist attacks, the massive amount of abducted children and the need for the community's help in solving the most recent murder case, I began thinking to myself of what the world be like when you arrived.

From that moment on I instantly became very protective of you and started making mental notes of do's and don'ts, both, for you and I. I remember the day your dad and I heard the rapid beating of your tiny heart for the first time. I wanted to express the joy I was feeling, but I was too speechless, and my mind had drawn a blank. All I knew was that that I was happier at the moment than I had ever been in my entire life. And just when I thought I couldn't feel any better, we had an ultrasound and your dad, and I saw you moving about in the womb. Everything was perfect.

You had ten little fingers and ten little toes. Your heart was beating as normal, and we found out that you were a little girl. Life was getting better by the minute. It wasn't too long after that when your father went on a shopping spree for you and came home with at least hundred dollars' worth of baby clothes. That was just the beginning of several shopping sprees he went on for you. You made him the happiest man in the world. I remember the night he said to me, "I like the name Desiree" and from that day forward we only called you Desi.

We had several conversations about your future, and we often wondered if you would be interested in learning how to play the compositions of Mozart on the piano or becoming the next Mary Lou Retton of gymnastics or if you would be brave and share the news of a loving God to all your peers. "Maybe we could persuade her to earn a medical or law degree from Harvard," I thought. We had so many hopes and dreams for you, and we wanted you to have the very best life we could give you. Out of all the plans, we had for you none of those plans included a funeral. When we learned

Transformation: From the Inside Out

of your death, it was like a ton of bricks had landed on our hearts, crushing it into a thousand pieces. After I had delivered you, I held you with tears flowing from my eyes. I began to tell you how pretty you were. "You look like your dad," I said. Then with my words falling from my mouth due to the crying I said: "I love you so much that if I could, I'd take you home with me just as you are." I know that sounds crazy, but I was that crazy over you. I forced myself to hand you back over to the nurse and that the last time your dad and I saw you. When I came home from the hospital, I looked up at the sky and told God that I didn't blame him for your death. However, there was another side of me that felt as though I had been teased. I felt as if someone had laid a twenty million dollars at my feet and snatched it back when I reached down to grab it. I nearly lost my mind. The only thing that helped me get through it was knowing that you are now in the arms of God.

When we found out that I was carrying you we gave you back to God and asked him to allow you to be a minister of some sort for him someday. Your name means to desire or long for. I believe that God honored our request and allowed you to become a ministering angel to carry the blessings to those who have desired and longed for something great to come their way. You will be missed; you brought us so much joy and laughter, and if we had ten more children you would always be the child that holds a special place in our hearts. May you continue to rest in peace and enjoy the loving embrace that comes from our heavenly Father, Love always,
Mommy and Daddy

This poem was something that I had written in 2003 for a memorial booklet in honor of my daughter Desiree, who was stillborn at about twenty weeks. When I wrote this piece, I was filled with mixed emotions. There was a part of me that was filled with hurt and anger and another part filled with guilt and sadness. I felt guilty because, to be honest, when I first found out that I was pregnant with her, I was angry. I had no desire to have any children. I was happy with my husband and his children that he had introduced me too. I had fallen in love with them and when he and I said, "I do", I claimed his kids as my own and was elated to have them in my life. So, when I learned that I was expecting, my husband did not say a word to me because he knew that I was heated. Well, after about two days of mentally fussing about it, I suddenly began to embrace the idea that I was going to be a mother. After all, there was nothing that I could do to change things. In my mind, when she died, I kept thinking that because I originally wanted to live a kid-free lifestyle, God was punishing me for my words.

The anger and hurt came because God knew that children were not a part of my future plans; and for Him to allow me to become pregnant and then lose the baby at the height of my joy simply crushed me. Moreover, when I did not think that things could get any worse, I was told that because my child was over twenty weeks, I had to hold a funeral for her and spend money that I was not prepared to relinquish. Oh yeah, I was furious! I was so mad at God during that period. I remember telling him that He and I had nothing to talk about *ever* again. That was a moment where I honestly did not care if I had a relationship with God or not.

I say this with much transparency because I know that several women have felt the same way and need to know that anger is a normal part of the healing process. Let's face it, who would not be upset when you have a child today, and tomorrow he or she is no longer with you. What's so puzzling is that a parent cannot adequately explain why they, out of all people, had to be the one to sit in front of their child's casket. If one would be truthful, it does not matter how old the child is when he or she dies or what the cause of death is, because losing a child hurts regardless of whether they are four weeks gestation or forty years of life. The fact remains that no good parent wants to outlive their child. The death of a child is a death like none other. The death of my daughter messed with my mind, and there were moments when I felt like I was going to go crazy. I have lost my mother, grandfather, and mother-in-law and was saddened by each of their passing. To this day, I miss each of them dearly and still shed a tear or two when they come to my mind; but losing my child is an unexplainable hurt.

Transformation: From the Inside Out

It is like my heart had just stopped beating, and nothing can shock it back into a beating rhythm.

During the process of my anger, I kept wondering what I did wrong to deserve losing my child. I could not wrap my mind around it for anything. However, my anger came upon me gradually. After Desiree had died, I tried to be a perfect soldier. The day of the funeral, I learned that my cousin's wife had just had a baby, and there were some complications with the child after delivery. So after the funeral, my husband and I left from the cemetery and went directly to the hospital to visit my cousin's newborn child. When we arrived at the hospital, I held the baby in my arms. I thought I had done something and mentally prided myself on the fact that I was holding a live baby without having a meltdown. At that time, it was a surreal moment for me, but I felt that I needed to be there for someone else in their moment of pain. From that moment, I thought I'd take things a step further and look at the newspaper and find the obituary of an infant and mail a card to the child's mother. I wanted my testimony to look really good. I wanted to let someone else know they were not alone in their grief, and it felt good to be a blessing to another person. However, that did not seem to be enough for me; it did not bring my child back nor did it restore my broken heart. I believe it was that moment that I started to transition into the angry stage. I felt that by me doing the "Christian" thing and putting my focus onto others meant that God would somehow turn around and miraculously bring me joy. However, what I learned was that I was trying to be a blessing prematurely, and it was not working for me at all. Now, allow me to take a commercial break for a PSA (Public Service Announcement): "Do not be quick to embrace everything you hear." Sometimes we hear testimonies of others, and we think that because it worked a certain way for one person, it will work the same for us. Okay, commercial is over. This is what I believed happened to me; I was operating on years of teachings and testimonies of others, thinking that if I did what someone said worked then my troubles would be over. Not so! For me, what I came to realize was that putting my focus onto others grief meant that I was in denial and masking my own sorrow. Instead of trying to be Superwoman, I should have connected with a support group and allowed someone to be Superwoman for me. I did not realize it at the time, but even though my reaching out came from the heart, it was too soon for me to minister to others and the spirit behind it was wrong. Therefore, it backfired on me, and I became angry.

Now, I am not saying that a woman who may be dealing with the loss of a child should not to be there for another person. I agree that there is a blessing in being a blessing, but sometimes we need to let the healing process take place before jumping out and being the rescuer of another person. Along with this, being knowledgeable of your own of boundaries; in other words, knowing when to step in and minister and when to step back and shut up. Again, what works for one does not work for all. Healing is not something that can be rushed through; it is a slow process with many phases and stages. For me, the stages were a refusal to accept, shock, confusion, denial, anger and recovery. I had to go through all those steps before I reached the healing part. Your stages and phases may look a little different, but regardless of how your steps towards healing look, allow the process to run its course, because you will have better results in the end.

As I was going through an array of emotions, I knew that for my mental health to get to a healthy state, I had to return to my normal. This meant that I had to go back to work, had to attend church and receive prayer and encouragement, and the greatest thing I needed to do was not be Superwoman. I had to stop looking for deceased children and hurting mothers. I had to pull back and admit to myself that I was doing something that I was not mentally or emotionally ready to handle. I had to regroup and surround myself with some "All the Way" people. "All the Way" people were those whom I trusted to take me all the way to my place of healing. I did not need those who would tell me, "Well, if you take care of God's business, he will take care of yours." I am not knocking the cliché', but I had tried that already, and it did more damage than good. I needed to be around people whom I knew would pull me back if they saw me going down a slippery slope, and let me grieve without making me feel that I was unspiritual.

My "All the Way" people prayed for me and encouraged me not to be afraid of trying for another child. Now, I know some women are not able to have another child, and if she could, there is no replacing of the one that was lost. However, a woman cannot be afraid to step into a motherly role and help nurture another child. My "All the Way" team were the ones who checked on me and did not allow me to stay in a state of depression. These are the same individuals who remained at my side, "All the Way" to the complicated pregnancy and delivery of my second daughter. Every hurting person needs some "All the Way" people on their team.

Sadly, there are some that have had to bury a child, and they just stop living. They go into hiding. They cut off their family and friends, and when they go to work, they are there only in body. When they come into contact with others, they refuse to listen to the words of encouragement and make excuses for why they cannot take the advice of others. They will sit around in their sadness and depression and watch everyone around live joyous and carefree lives. The heart breaking part is that if they do have a circle of friends, they are the "Half Way" people. Those who keep a group of "Half Way" people nearby will never heal.

This reminds me of the scripture in John 5:1-7, where it reads, "After this there was a feast of the Jews, and Jesus went up to Jerusalem. Now there is in Jerusalem by the Sheep *Gate* a pool, which is called in Hebrew, Bethesda, having five porches. In these lay a great multitude of sick people, blind, lame, paralyzed, waiting for the moving of the water. For an angel went down at a certain time into the pool and stirred up the water; then whoever stepped in first, after the stirring of the water, was made well of whatever disease he had. Now a certain man was there who had an infirmity thirty-eight years. When Jesus saw him lying there and knew that he already had been *in that condition* a long time, He said to him, "Do you want to be made well?" The sick man answered Him, "Sir,

I have no man to put me into the pool when the water is stirred up; but while I am coming, another steps down before me."

Now, there is a lot that one can take away from that passage of scripture, but what I want to focus on is this man who was sick for thirty-eight years and had a "Half Way" team in his corner. They took the time to bring him to the pool, and when the waters stirred they were not around to put him in the pool. They "Half Way" did the job. They allowed him to sit and watch others receive their healing and go on to enjoy their lives. There are so many women that have lost a child and unfortunately have surrounded themselves with "Half Way" friends. They will only take you so far, and will leave you hanging when it matters most. They can see that you are not the same person that you were before the tragic loss, and are aware that you need some additional coaching and help. However, instead of them helping you get to your place of healing; they leave you at the "half way" mark.

When you are dealing with a loss of a child, do not surround yourself with a "Half Way" team that will allow you to stay in the state of grief forever. Align yourselves with those who will take you beyond the halfway mark and escort you to a place a healing. Remember, processing through pain is slow, but there is an expiration period. "Half Way" people will allow you to go "All the Way" beyond your shelf life.

I opened my story with a reflective poem because my writing was the beginning of my healing. It was my way of bringing closure to my pain. I had to take a moment to look back so that I could go forward. I needed to do something sensible and healthy to help me get through a moment that I never thought in a thousand years I would have to face. Looking back is okay, but do not get stuck in the memories. Allow the healing process to do what it needs to do for you, and find your therapy. My therapy was writing and my "All the Way" crew. Your therapy can be something else, but make sure you have an "All the Way" team in the process. I think of my Desi often, and have gone to her burial site and cleaned the headstone. However, I do not get stuck there; I keep it moving. I keep it moving for my surviving children and my grandchildren, my husband and those who do not need me to be a Superwoman but for those who need me to an "All the Way" woman for them. For those of you that are still questioning why your son or your daughter is no longer with you, "Wow," I wish I had an answer for you. What I can say is that even though you never get over the death, you can return to a life of normalcy. It may take a while, but it can be done. Take each step slowly and before you know it, you will find yourself in a place of complete healing.

Autograph Page

Pastor Michele Miller

Transformation: From the Inside Out

Transformation: From the Inside Out

About the Author

Pastor Notoshia D. Howard

Pastor Notoshia D. Howard was born and raised in Indianapolis, Indiana to William Sullivan and the late Denise Oxendine-Sullivan on October 9, 1971. She was raised by her late grandparents William and Marie Sullivan. Notoshia attended school in the Indianapolis public school system. She holds her B.A. Degree in Liberal Arts from I.U.P.U.I., in Indianapolis. She also holds a Master's Degree in Ministry with a concentration in ministerial leadership from Indiana Wesleyan University. On July 25, 2016, she will return to school with intentions of receiving another Master's Degree in Theology, and on from there pursue a PhD in Theology.

In July of 2000, she received her license to preach the gospel under the leadership of Pastor Joseph M. Tunstill, pastor of Joshua Missionary Baptist Church. In 2009, Notoshia and her Husband Pastor Eddie Howard, founded and planted Freewill Christian Ministries Church. Then in 2010, she was ordained by Apostle Jacqueline Powell at Augusta Christian Church/ Powerhouse International Ministries. In 2012, Pastor Toshia travelled to Togo West Africa on a mission trip, with the Glory Connection.

In 2006, Pastor T, as she is called, published her first book called *Inheritance, Leaving a Rich Foundation for Your Children and Grandchildren* and in 2008 her second book called *Women Still*

Transformation: From the Inside Out

Struggling to Preach: The Atmosphere is Ready, was released and in 2010 *Has the World Gone to Whoredom on God?* Also in 2010, Pastor Toshia founded/planted Howard Publishing Press LLC., where she has published other authors' written work. She is also the managing editor and publisher of *Sister2Sistah*.

In 2016, God gave Pastor Toshia the vision for this book, *Sister2Sistah* and the people whom would help to carry out this vision. Prophetically spoken, this is not just a book but also a movement to get our sisters and women back to the feet of Jesus.

Notoshia has been married to Pastor Eddie D. Howard Sr., for nineteen years and together they share five children: Eddie Jr., Christopher, Shrieka, Genesis, Solomon, and two grandchildren: Xavier (Tuttabutt) and Mayson (Nanagirl).

Transformation: From the Inside Out

Acknowledgements

First, I AM INDEBTED TO GOD! I thank Him for His loving kindness. I thank Him for all He has done, is doing and for what He will continue to do.

To my husband, Pastor Eddie, I thank you for your love and support, and for all the moments that we have shared together, including our gray skies and our bright sunshine. I thank you for your continuous encouragement every time I undertake an assignment from God. No one has ever loved and supported me like you have, and for that, I am eternally grateful. Not only do we get to spend this Earthly life together, but also the eternal life together. Our headstones will be right next to each other (inside joke).

To my children, whom I love dearly: Eddie Jr., Christopher, Shrieka, Genesis, and Solomon, I praise and thank God for each of you every day. To my grandbabies: Xavier (Tuttabutt) and Mayson (Nanagirl).

I dedicate this book to Pastors Bobby and Martha Kirkley of White Horse Christian Center for their continuous insight, love and support.

I dedicate this book to Apostle Jacquelyn Powell and Pastor Randy of Augusta Christian Church and Powerhouse International Ministries. Thank you for the love, support and consistent teaching.

I dedicate this book to my daughters, sisters, aunts and women everywhere, I pray that this book is planted right next to your Bible for daily encouragement and support.

A special thank you to Prophetess Rachel Sanders (BFF) and all the authors that told their most personal stories, to help another sister. God's word is true and His promises and blessings are for you!

Transformation: From the Inside Out

Transformation: From the Inside Out

Rejected but Anointed

Broken

How did I get to this place in God, this place that feels so good, and feels so right? A place that is stable in Him, my Creator and my Father. A position that is not based off man's interpretation of me, but the work that God has done within me, from the inside out. My identity is not based off what manor woman can and cannot do for me. Have I obtained perfection yet? Nope, not by a long shot, but I am growing, and I am neither who I was last year nor last month. To me, it is a personal day by day process, where I choose to walk in my own shoes and not anyone else's. You see, my sistah, God mandated for us to walk in total freedom, healing and destiny, and not for us to continue on broken, busted and disguised. There was a time when I walked in all three of these verbs: broken in Spirit, busted in attitude and disguised in my skin.

Nevertheless, today, I have made a choice to allow God to heal my heart and the most secret hurts and pains that I have chosen to carry and nurse since childhood. I say chosen to carry, because even though we have been given freedom and total victory, there is a breakdown between the knowing it and the walking in it. There is a disconnect between what God has already done for us, and what we are supposed to do in order to continue on to get the blessing. We have been conditioned and told that God loves us and will never leave us or forsake us, and even though his word provides for us over a thousand promises, we are too lazy to find the conditions of the promises and work the conditions in order to walk in the blessings. What I am saying is that we all have problems, troubles and circumstances, but we don't have to get wet in the rain if we have an umbrella within arm's reach.

A couple months ago, my husband brought some light to a dark path that many of us are walking alone in and do not want to acknowledge. He said, "We all have a story. My story may not be your story and your story may not be my story, but we all have a story. Whether it be good or bad, God is the judge of that story."

Transformation: From the Inside Out

And I got to thinking how people, in general, will zero in on the bad story of a person's life versus the good story of their life. In addition, because we know how society is, we will try and keep that bad story covered up. No matter how much pain and suffering it may cause us internally, all because we want to appear as though everything is okay, when in actuality it is not.

I have come to myself as the rich man's son did in Luke 15:11-32. I now know that matters of the heart are meant to be healed and not covered with a bandage. I know that sometimes we can hurt so much on the inside that it will make us sick on the outside, and sometimes even destroy other relationships that God has for us.

I remember many years ago meeting a friend for lunch and she told me that God's hand has been upon my life since I was two years old. However, throughout my life I never felt that God's hand was upon me. Here I was at the age of twenty-one still trying to find myself. Still trying to find out who I was and where I belonged. Even though I had a family that loved me, I have always and still felt that something was missing. Going from relationship to relationship, from hurt to hurt and from one pain to another. Yet I was still pushing and smiling while bleeding on the inside. On the outside, I looked as though everything was all good most of the time. You know how we do it. We put the makeup on and we put the nice clothing on, and we look the part. Yet, it is hard trying to keep a smile on your face while knowing you're trying to fake and imagine that everything is well.

The life I wanted to live, the life I thought every child is due, really is not the way it always ends up being. I remember growing up and constantly saying to myself, when I get grown, I am going to marry the man of my dreams, have two kids, have a big house with a white picket fence, and a dog out front. Rich and blessed! Doesn't that sound good? Yet, it didn't happen that way. Only to end up still trying to find myself, in debt from college, with five children, an awesome husband, and a church that keeps me busy. What I have grown to find out, is that our flesh can desire one thing, and our spirit man can desire something very different; and because our spirit man is that inner being where God resides, He knows what our true desires are. God knew I was going to need a husband that would love me unconditionally. He knew I would need a physically strong man to cover me and encourage me when I accepted my calling to ministry and felt like I could not go on. He knew I needed children that would rise up and call me blessed, and that love my cooking. He knew I would need grandchildren that would grab me around the neck and say, "Nana, I love you and miss you." Out of all the hurt and pain in life, my husband, children and grandchildren have brought me unspeakable joy!

    We all go through different things in life. Some things we bring on ourselves and other things God allows for His purpose and destiny for our life, but that does not mean that God does not love us. When we are going through each struggle, we can only see the middle of the problem versus the purpose of the problem or the outcome. Many people get to a place of brokenness, which is caused by false expectation of people, places and things. We begin to carry and even nurse the hurt that we have experienced. It's almost like an open wound that never heals properly because we keep allowing it to be infected versus healed. The spirit of brokenness brings on the spirit of fear, rejection, mental attacks, low self-esteem, character issues and false-responsibility. On the inside, our heart is cracked, and it feels like we are going to crumble or lose our mind at any minute. We feel damaged, fractured and live a crippled life. In other words, we become defective on our way to being demolished. I know this is a mouth full, but I will unpack later. Nevertheless, I promise you that in all the rubble, through all the tears and shame, there is help.

    For many years and for many reasons I was broken. To be honest, at some points in my life, I was mentally messed up. I remember as a child at my grandmother's house, I was having anger issues and banging my head on the wall, because I was not able to release my hurt and pain of not having a mother. Yet, my grandmother seemed to understand and even in the midst of the hurt and growing pains, she reciprocated it with love and nourishment.

Nevertheless, there are some things that just cannot replace the love of a biological mother. No matter how right, wrong or messed up momma is, that's my momma. No matter how much my grandmother did, or how much I had or was given, it never seemed to be enough to fill the empty whole that was in my heart. I always knew and felt in my heart that it was just natural to have a mother. It was something that everyone had and who every child lived with. I cannot remember my mother nor can I tell you what her touch was like, yet there was a yearning for something that was just natural. Often people say, "momma's baby and daddy's maybe", but that's not true, because it's natural to have a mother and father. That's how God designed it.

My mother and father got married early in life. Way before my mother died, my father's mother took me from them and raised me as her own. My mother died when she was about seventeen or eighteen and I was two. As I now write about her death, I am writing from a place of total healing. I know that as she was responsible for the life she lived, I am responsible for the life I live. I don't want my children to feel how I felt because my mother was not there. As I write this, I am writing from a place of peace, as I know that she is not coming back and that she did not die because of me, but because of the way she chose to live her life.

I write from a place of purpose and desperation to be there at every step for my children and grandchildren. From time to time, I look at the relationship that I have with my daughter Genesis and wish that it could be three generations fellowshipping together; but God quickly reminds me of the joy that He has given me right in front of my eyes. The Son will always bring joy, peace and love if I focus on Him.

The Spirit of Rejection

While growing up I used to think *this is not normal to live life without a mother*. I was living life walking around with a "what if" syndrome. Timid and mean, walking around looking like I had a permanent lemon in my mouth. Fighting on the inside, trying to love myself, whom I thought was unlovable. Heck, sometimes I didn't even like myself. I always felt that this timidity came from being left uncovered as a child, that it is the mother and father's right, duty and assignment from God to protect and provide for their child. Moreover, here I was, a child trying to fight for myself and make my voice be heard in a world that seemed to take no interest in what I had to say.

I remember sitting in high school and daydreaming that my mother had faked her death or that she was sick and that at the right time she would walk back into my life. At first, I would be upset, but then it would be as though we had never missed any time together. She would love me unconditionally and apologize for not being there for me.

I remember dreaming that we would be sitting and talking about her grandchildren and discussing how they are growing up. I remember thinking *what would I do if I ran into her on the street or in the store*? Or, *what if she is not really dead but has another family*? For some reason, even though I had her death certificate and my family told me her story, I just could not come to grips mentally that she was not there and was never coming back. It's not like I knew her and we had a relationship and then she passed because she was sick or something. I never knew my mother! And yet, it didn't stop the feelings and the 'what if' questions that were flowing in my mind and heart. I think sometimes we become zombies—not the scary movie zombies—but the cold hearted, unfeeling zombies where the pain does not register. Or maybe like a robot, where we go on as business as usual on the outside.

For many years, I had thoughts or felt that she didn't want me or that I messed up her life. I wondered about if I could just see her one more time, what would my questions and comments be? I am talking about my biological mother, the one that gave birth to me and the one that held me in her arms. I am talking about my mother who died early, a woman I never knew, yet felt connected to. A woman that was not there when I gave birth to my children, got married, accepted my calling to preach, graduated high school and college. She was never there!

Time and time again going to doctor's office visits and the doctor would ask, "Does anyone on your mother's side have diabetes, heart problems, cancer and etc.?", and the look on my doctor's face when I say I don't know as she died when I was little. In addition, the feelings that would swell up in me when I would say she is dead.

Do you want me to define rejection or can you see how the spirit of rejection alone with guilt, shame and abandonment had set in? Not to mention, feelings of no identity and the question of where do I belong or fit in at? One of the main problems that I struggled with was my identity. I needed to identify with my mother, I needed to feel her, see her and touch her. I needed her hug, her kiss and for her to tell me that everything would be alright; I needed that confirmation and affirmation. I needed that from her and never received it. We often talk about the Father's blessing, and I understand that wholeheartedly, but what about the physical mother's blessing? What I am saying is that there were some things I needed to learn from her. There were some things I needed her to speak into my spirit man or my womanhood, things I felt that only a mother could give a daughter. Many nights I cried myself to sleep and many nights I could not sleep at all because I was angry at God for taking her and angry at her because she was not there. Even in my adult life, when I would read Psalms 27:10, "When my father and mother forsake me, then the Lord will take me up" (KJV). I used to be angry and say in my heart to God, "How can you take me up, when you are the one that took her?" I was angry and mad at the same time and questioned God about her death and her not being there.

Transformation: From the Inside Out

I used to think *how could God love me, how could He care about what I was going through*? Didn't He know that I needed her? Didn't He know that my heart ached and hurt at the same time? Could He feel my loneliness and yearning to be loved? I have carried this rejection for almost thirty years, and nursed it as if it were a newborn baby.

I believe that God really knows how much we can take, therefore, He knows when enough is enough. When we finally and truly come to ourselves and say to God, "God, I am at the end of my rope and if you don't help me I will not make it." This becomes a life or death move on our behalf, and this was where I was, a life or death situation. I chose to live and give God a chance to heal me from the inside out.

Last year, I preached a sermon called, "Don't Make a Pit Stop a Home". I spoke about the life of Joseph, and how he had all these different pit stops and he could have made each one a home. Yet instead, he learned from that pit stop and moved to the next pit stop. He didn't make a home for his problems to dwell in. For example, when his brothers sold him into slavery (pit stop) and when he was thrown into jail (pit stop). He moved from one pit stop to the next to get to his destiny, which was to become the second in charge under Pharaoh and to save his family when famine came. I know now that every pit stop (struggle, problem or trial) is simply that, just a pit stop. God always does what is best for us even, if it sometimes hurts! Even if He has to remove people so you can see Him clearly (Isaiah 6).

Anointed

I now know that God has anointed my life and ordered my footsteps, and no devil in Hell can destroy it. God is for me and has been all my life. He makes decisions based off what is best for our future, our destiny and His Glory. I believe if I had not gone through the things I have been through, I would not be the person I am today. The mother, wife or the God fearing woman that I am. I love God with all my heart, soul, mind, strength and all that is within me. I cannot see myself ever walking away from God, because He is my mother and father, and there is no one better for me to lean on that will always be there. People die, people walk out on you, people turn against you, people talk about you, but God will never leave nor forsake you. One of the other authors said, "If He did it before, He can do it again". She is so right, and sometimes He throws a little extra in there, as He truly knows the desires of our hearts!

I remember at the end of 2011, when Apostle Jacquelyn Powell asked if I wanted to join her pastoral team called the Glory Connection and travel to Togo, West Africa. My first reaction and response was "Oh, my God! Not me! Thank you God!" I was excited and cheerful at the same time, but then I began to think about the flight there. I had never been on an airplane before, now I choose for my first flight to travel across the world. It took three airplanes to get there and three airplanes to get back home, and fear began to set in. As we began to prepare for our trip, money became an issue. Here I had a free trip to Africa with no spending money. Nevertheless, when God has destined you for greatness, He opens doors for you to get and have what you need in order to do what He has called you to do. As soon as 2012 hit, I began to get a lot of preaching engagements, which allowed me to put those offerings aside for spending money for our trip to Africa. Along with my husband, who blessed me off on my trip, and made sure I had everything I needed. It was a trip that God so much wanted me to take. To see His glory and power, and how people in another country worship and praise Him. To see how we need to hunger and thirst for Him and to seek His face. This trip made me realize how blessed we are here in America, and yet we have too much that's blocking us and taking us away from what we were created to do— and that is to worship Him. You cannot worship without the word, and many of us are too busy to read and meditate on the word daily.

When God anoints and calls you, He always provides the means for you to undertake and do what He has called you to do. One thing I have found out about God in all these years is that He is faithful and true to His word. Not only is He faithful, but also He always provides for His children. After forty-three years, I now realize that I do carry a special anointing, one that many do not carry. I believe that our character must be able to withstand the amount of power that God gives us, unless we become destructive to others and ourselves.

    I had been preaching and teaching for years. Years of spending time with God, waiting and listening for Him to drop golden nuggets into my spirit man, which would change my life forever. I always knew that God was faithful to His word. With the type of foundation and upbringing in the church that I had, I knew there was more to God than what I had been experiencing. I knew that when the scriptures read, "O taste and see that the Lord is good" (Psalms 34:8, KJV). It really meant that God is good on this side, and that He has even more benefits and blessings for us when we get over to glory!

    I remember one of my younger cousins use to lead a song called, "Thee Anointing". It's funny how you reflect back and realize how you can listen to a song or to sermons about the anointing, yet never really knew what or who the anointing was. We sung about being filled with the Holy Spirit, yet we didn't operate in the Spirit as we ought to have been. Now when I hear or sing that song, all I can do is cry, because the lyrics to that song are so true. I remember when I first started speaking in tongues. Here I was, a Baptist from birth, yet knowing that there was still more to Jesus than what I already knew and experienced. I had begun to get a hunger and thirst for more of God. I had met a woman at work, who always had unspeakable joy. She, in turn, introduced me to an older woman that helped birth me into speaking in tongues. I remember I had got off work early and met her at her home church. She introduced me to her pastor, who is an awesome man of God! At our second meeting, as I was going into the building, I ran into the pastor, and brought him a bottle of Propel water. I told him it was good, and he in turn took it, and said, "Make sure you enjoy your spiritual water." Ever since that encounter with the fire of God, of course, that woman, I have not been right since. After leaving their church, every word that came out of my mouth that day was in tongues. There was such a fulfilling on the inside, a burning sensation, with unspeakable joy.

Therefore, after that meeting, I began to visit the bookstores. I began to buy different books on the Holy Spirit, healing and deliverance, speaking in tongues, and signs and miracles. I never knew I would be going back to those same books fourteen years later, as a pastor, helping someone else get free. Total freedom and liberty is being able to lay aside your agenda and immediately change to God's agenda in a split second. That day, God interrupted my life for the good! During the daytime, I was studying His word and at night, I was waiting to hear Him or see what He wanted to show me. As questions began to arise in my mind, I wished I had someone to talk to about it. About why my right palm would get hot all of the sudden, or why my whole body would be hot some nights, as if I had a fever, and I was not even sick. Then, sometimes, my forehead will get hot and I can feel a presence upon me. I am talking about the supernatural power of God.

In 2013, I was invited to speak in Illinois at a women's conference, and it was called The School of the Holy Spirit. I had preached and taught for years at my home church and away, yet this was something very different that God was doing in me. I was asked to do a workshop dealing with the Holy Spirit. I was to teach on whom the Holy Spirit is, what does He do, by what means does He do it? There is one thing that I have learned about God and know for sure, and that is that He loves unity and diversity, which is how it will be in heaven. At this women's conference, God took women from different ethnic groups and of different ages, and allowed us to go into the Holy of Holies. When I say the Holy of Holies, I am saying we gathered in a corporate location or church, as our spirit men came together as one. People came to have an encounter with God! Women came to get answers from God, but most importantly, we came to meet the Father. Oh, boy was the Father there. Both days I was completely prostrate before God, and could not do anything but cry and worship. That Saturday morning,

Transformation: From the Inside Out

I was down under the bench just crying out before God, all the way up until it was my turn to speak.

Now, let me back up to get you to where I need you to be. A couple weeks prior to the gathering, I had been reading and meditating on Act 1:8, "But ye shall receive power, after that the Holy Ghost is come upon you: and ye shall be witnesses unto me both in Jerusalem, and in all Judaea, and in Samaria, and unto the uttermost part of the Earth." I had been asking God what He wanted me to say. All week I kept looking at that verse and other verses that God would drop into my spirit man. After service on Friday night, I sat up and read over my notes that I had previously prepared, and then just began to get quiet before Him. At 5:00 A.M. that morning, God woke me up and took me to Genesis 1:1, John 1:1, Hebrews 10:5-6, John 14:20 and John 15:4, "That all of the Godhead is within us. That the only way we can demonstrate His charisma and imitate His glory, is that He has to live on the inside of us. That God, Jesus and the Holy Spirit are one and that when the Holy Spirit comes on the inside of us, then we become one with God." That does not mean that we are exactly like God, but what it does mean is that we have some mighty Holy Ghost power working on the inside of us. He equips us, edifies us, enlightens us, enables us, empowers us, energizes us and endorses us. My sistah, He has endorsed me and He has endorsed you. God has given us the seal of approval.

To get and keep the type of anointing that God has given us, we have to walk through the fire or the process to realize that all we need or ever needed was already there inside of us, we just had to believe in Him and live out the conditions that the word of God provides us.

That weekend at the revival, God blew my mind! I found a place in God that I never knew existed! It was not about the people or the location, it was about the expectation that was down on the inside of me and the pouring out that I did before Him. It is one thing to read the Word from God, but when God brings revelation to you and you begin to see things differently, it changes your life. That day, God allowed me to know Him in a deeper and more intimate way. Intimacy is what God wants from us. He wants us to be intimate with Him, sharing with Him our deepest thoughts, struggles and heartaches. Even though He already knows them, He wants us to share them with Him.

    I remember when I was in high school, and in our history class the teacher said, "God wants to be intimate with us." Another student yelled out, "I don't want to have sex with God!" I remember thinking and actually saying out loud, "I don't want to have sex with God either, but it's not about sex." Nevertheless, what the teacher was saying is that God wants us to perfect our relationship with Him, just as a husband and wife are joined together as one. God wants that secret place where no one else abides but Him. It's in that secret place that we get directions, comfort and revelation about who we really are and what we are called to do. On July 6, 2014, I preached a sermon called; *You Are Anointed for the Assignment God Has Called You To*. My sister, "He is worth it, and so are you!"

Transformation: From the Inside Out

Autograph Page

Pastor Notoshia D. Howard

Transformation: From the Inside Out

Contact information for Authors

Kizzy Hayes — hayeskizzy@yahoo.com

Schurronda White — schurronda.white@g3tp.com

Brittany Sullivan — sullivanb21@gmail.com

Trease Sears — treasesears@yahoo.com

Marian Steele — m.steele56@sbcglobal.net

Roberta Bell — robertabelltraining@gmail.com

Pastor Michele Miller — smithmill@hotmail.com

Peggy Finkton — pafinkton@sbcglobal.net

howardpublishing@sbcglobal.net
www.howardpublishing.com

Howard Publishing Press LLC is a Christian publishing company, ordained to publish the gift that God has given to those who are called to proclaim their message through writing. It is our purpose to motivate and assist in spreading the gospel of Jesus Christ by aiding God's people in fulfilling their God-given purpose. As a destiny helper, our purpose is also to help authors publish their material at an efficient, low cost. We are a self-publishing company, publishing books for those who do not have the time or opportunity to do the legwork that is needed to produce quality work at an affordable cost.